FILM
TO
FREEDOM

Turn Your Passion for Videography
Into a 6-Figure Income

GRANT BURKS

THE FREE FILM
TO FREEDOM
COMPANION COURSE!

This book contains links to resources that will help you on your journey to scaling your videography business to a full-time income. All of these resources, along with bonus video content I have created for you, can be found by logging in to the companion course. To access the free course, go to the link below:

www.videography-university.com/course

This book is dedicated to you.
All of you who have dreams of achieving personal
and financial success running your own videography business.

You can do it.

I hope this book helps you make your dreams a reality.

- Grant Burks

"Freedom lies
in being bold."

—Robert Frost

TABLE OF CONTENTS

Section 5: The 3-Phase Approach to 6-Figure Sales

Section 6: Next Steps

Section 1

Video to Victory

This book is meant to serve as a guide for those looking to build a videography business into a full-time career and ultimately live a more rewarding and fulfilling life. In this book, I have condensed my seven years of knowledge in the industry and the lessons that I've learned building my videography business to a full-time career and six-figure income. This book will be focused less on the technical aspects of videography (if you want to learn the technical aspects of videography, you can check out my YouTube channel at www.youtube.com/GrantBurks) and more on the marketing skills, sales tactics, and mindset necessary to scale your business to six figures.

As we'll talk about later in the book, time is your most valuable asset when it comes to building your business. For that reason, I don't want to waste your time. Depending on where you're at in your journey and where your interests lie, you may want to skip around in the book or only key in on certain chapters. Here is a breakdown of how I recommend you read this book given different points in the process of scaling your business:

1. *$0 in Sales.* You are passionate and curious about starting a videography business but have not yet taken any steps to begin the journey.
   a. Start in Section 1, Chapter 1: Camera to Cash, which tells my story.
   b. If you don't want to hear how I grew my business to six figures, skip to Section 2: Mastering Your Mindset.
2. *$1–$50,000 in Sales.* You have a camera, and you've shot a few projects, but you're struggling with how to grow and where to go from here.
   a. I recommend reading Section 1, Chapter 1: Camera to Cash, Chapter 2: Mastering Your Mindset, and Chapter 3: Nailing Your Niche. Next you might consider skipping Section 4: Building Your Brand and reading Section 5: The 3-Phase Approach to 6-Figure Sales.
   b. If you don't want to hear how I grew my business to six figures, skip to Section 2: Mastering Your Mindset, and then continue with the above order.
3. *$50,000–$99,999 in Sales:* You've built a strong business, you have a solid foundation, but you simply need the sales process to help you pass the six-figure mark.

    a. I recommend skipping directly to Section 5: The 3-Phase Approach to 6-Figure Sales.

    b. You might still find value in Section 1 where I tell my story and Section 2 about mastering your mindset. Consider reading these two sections and then jumping to Section 5.

4. *$100,000+ in Sales*: Congratulations, my friend, you've done it! You've built a business that has likely already allowed you to achieve your "why." (Read Section 2, Chapter 5 if you're not sure what your "why" is.) If you're at this point and you're struggling to find processes to continue earning more sales, I recommend reading Section 5: The 3-Phase Approach to 6-Figure Sales.

Wherever you're at in your journey, I want you to know that building a full-time career out of videography is possible, it's attainable, and it's probable if you take the right steps to make it happen. My goal with this book is to equip you with the tactics to get there. These are the same steps that I took to scale my videography business from $16,000 as a side-job while working a 9-to-5 to $114,000 and a full-time career within a span of three years. The entire journey from when I bought my first camera to when I built my business to a full-time career and a six-figure income took seven years. With the steps I teach in this book, you can do it within 10 to 12 months.

To break down topics in more detail and provide you with more value, I have created a free companion course for this book. This companion course is called Film to Freedom and can be found at www.videography-university.com/course. Before continuing with this book, I highly recommend going to www.videography-university.com/course and to receive your free login. You will find links throughout this book to the Film to Freedom companion course that provide you access to documents, videos, and other resources that will help you along your journey of building your business. The Film to Freedom book and companion course will provide you with all of the steps you need to build your videography business to a six-figure income.

For those who want to go further faster or want guidance along the way to building their business, my team and I have created a program called Videography University. Students of Videography University get one-on-one coaching to help them in any areas they need, access to our private Facebook Group with other students where you can ask questions about challenges you are facing, and additional training videos breaking down the technical side of videography/video production. If you want to learn more about Videography University to see if it's a good fit for you, book a free consultation call with my team at www.videography-university.com/apply.

Chapter 1

CAMERA TO CASH

Two months after my twentieth birthday, I made a decision that turned my world upside down. As a kid, one of my favorite things in life was watching movies. I am a firm believer that stories are one of the most powerful tools in the world, and the way that movies bring stories to life is something that has always inspired me. Having a love for movies, two months after my twentieth birthday, I decided to purchase my first camera: a $1,200 Canon 70D.

I wanted to see what stories I could tell with a camera and discover ways to recreate some of the same movie magic that I saw on the big screen. At the time, I didn't really know what I wanted to do with my life. I was in my second year of college studying business at The Ohio State University, but I wasn't sure what the end goal was for me. I loved film, but I had always been told you couldn't make a career out of it, and I loved business, but it was really the entrepreneurial side that I loved, which sadly, I wasn't getting much of at school.

Two months after my camera arrived in the mail, my buddy, Kyler Holland, asked me if I wanted to help him on a project. Kyler was a friend at OSU who also had a love for video. In fact, he had turned his love for video into a YouTube Channel of over 250,000 subscribers where he taught tutorials on video editing. (You can check out his YouTube channel linked here: www.youtube.com/@THEKYLERHOLLAND)

"Hey, man! I have a wedding a couple hired me to shoot this weekend. Would you want to be my second shooter for the day? I'll teach you some things about your camera, and you'll get a nice dinner!" Kyler said.

Being a poor college student at the time, a free meal was more than enough compensation for me. Learning from Kyler about how to better use my camera? Icing on the cake.

"Absolutely, man! I'm in," I told him with undeniable excitement in my voice.

That Saturday morning Kyler picked me up, and I was on my way to shoot my very first project. Flexing my video skills throughout the day was exhilarating. It was a rush every time I composed a shot, hit "record," and reviewed the playback to see what I had created. I felt like a director constructing my first film. The bridal party was a joy to work with. The bride and groom, beyond thankful for our efforts throughout the day. The day was a blast, and I learned more than I ever could have imagined.

After we wrapped up for the day, we headed home. After we pulled into my apartment complex, I thanked Kyler for an awesome day and grabbed the door handle to get out of the car.

"Hold on!" Kyler said.

I turned back, as Kyler reached into his pocket, pulled out a crisp $100 bill, and handed it to me with a smile. "Thanks for all your work today, buddy!"

I went up to my apartment room, opened the door, threw all of my gear on the floor, sat on my bed, and pulled that $100 bill out of my wallet. I stared at it, and as Mr. Benjamin Franklin stared back at me, I saw a new opportunity in life. I was just paid very real money capturing video with my camera. I now understood what I wanted to do in life: I wanted to run my own videography business.

Chapter 2

SELF-DOUBT IS
SELF-DESTRUCTION

One of my favorite quotes from the great Henry Ford is as follows: "Whether you think you can or can't, you're right." Self-confidence is the key to success. If you believe you can accomplish something, you will inevitably find a way to make it happen. If you tell yourself you can't, you're undoubtedly going to fail. In my senior year of college, I allowed doubt to control my future.

In my last three years in college, I continued to take on videography jobs that came my way while I took classes. All of these projects came about through word of mouth as friends and family told their friends about me. The projects were a mix of weddings and a few small projects for local businesses. I was earning money and loved the work I was doing. My last year of college, I was getting closer to graduating, and I had friends and family asking me, "Where are you going to work after college?"

I was scared to tell them my dreams of running my own videography business. It was a bit of a unique path compared to most of my friends and family who went to college and got a job working for a company. I could not point to someone and say, "Look! They did it. They found success in doing this thing they love." I was too ashamed of the judgment I would receive from pursuing this alternative path in life.

Eight months out from my graduation date, I was shooting an event for a small business that had come from a friend of a friend. I was being paid $500 to capture a conference for an industry organization of lawyers. A few months' worth of rent for a poor college student. There was a photographer at the event capturing photos of attendees and speakers. He looked to be around his mid-thirties and was a bit disheveled.

I figured he might be able to give me advice, given he appeared to be making a career with his camera. I sat down next to him during the lunch break and struck up a conversation. After a bit of small talk, I asked him the big question, "So I'm actually in college right now, and I'll be graduating next semester. I haven't really told anybody yet, but I'm hoping to pursue running my own videography business full-time post-graduation. Any advice for me?"

He looked me in the eyes and with a mouth full of food said, "Don't do it." My heart sank. "I do this to make a few bucks mostly. You'll never make more than what you spend on equipment."

I allowed the words of a shoddy part-time photographer spoken through a mouthful of ham sandwich to shape my post-graduation plans. Corporate 9-to-5, here I come.

Chapter 3
UNCAPPED POTENTIAL

I graduated and started a job on the operations side of a healthcare IT company. The job checked all of the boxes for most people—good pay, great benefits, fun environment—but I was left feeling unfulfilled. I felt like a prisoner in the 9-to-5 world. I was thankful for the job I was given and the paycheck I was provided, but I felt as though I was a slave to my work. I had to be available at all times to answer questions, I needed to make sure that my boss was satisfied with the work that I was producing, and I was making the same paycheck every week, no matter how hard I worked.

I had a great boss, my company provided more flexibility than the companies most of my friends worked at, and I wasn't living on ramen noodles, but I felt like there had to be something more.

I found myself thinking back on the joys I felt running my own videography business in college. I'd had so much fun doing something I loved, and it had been exhilarating feeling like I'd been building my own business and had uncapped potential.

After a few months of feeling down, I decided to open myself up to opportunities to do videography projects on the side. It could be a nice way to earn a few extra bucks, and maybe it would bring some of that joy back that I was missing. After shooting a few weddings in college, I felt this could be a good way to jump back into the world of videography. I created an Instagram account for my wedding videography business and began posting clips from the weddings I shot in college. I tagged everyone I knew in the bridal parties and posted clips and stills from the footage three days a week for a span of three months.

A few weeks went by and wedding videography inquiries started hitting my email inbox. By the end of three months, I had booked around five weddings for the coming year. Once word spread again that I was doing videography, I had friends reaching out, saying their companies or someone they knew was looking for a reliable videographer. I started booking corporate jobs that I could capture after work and on weekends. Most were small jobs shooting social media content for small business or solo entrepreneurs, but I rediscovered the passion that I had missed and I was making decent money as well.

As time went on, the projects grew. After my first full calendar year working at my 9-to-5 and doing videography on the side, I made $43,308.69 from my 9-to-5 and $16,564.00

doing videography on the side. Not a bad deal making $16,000 dollars on the side doing something you love.

The next year, things continued to grow. I was doing well at my 9-to-5 and was lucky enough to be promoted to a new role, which resulted in a raise. At the same time, my videography side-business continued to grow as well and at a much faster rate. After spending a year honing the sales process and shooting process for my wedding videography business, I was able to run this part of my business on autopilot. I was booking my calendar out a year in advance for weddings and had more inquiries than I could handle. I was also shooting more corporate projects for small business and solo entrepreneurs. After my second full year in my 9-to-5 and doing videography on the side, I made $56,263.37 from my 9-to-5 and $47,992.00 from videography on the side. This is when I realized the power of uncapped potential.

At the start of the next year, I received an inquiry for a videography project that would be my biggest project to date. I met with the marketing director for the company multiple times until I had a complete understanding of the project, drafted up a proposal, and with nervous fingers hit "send."

Click

The next day, I looked in my inbox to find an unread message. "This looks great! We would like to move forward with the project."

I couldn't believe it.

That day I inked my first five-figure deal. In two days of shooting and three days of editing, I was going to make $12,000. (In Section 5 we'll talk about the sales tactics that helped make this happen.) It would take me almost three months working my full-time job to make that same amount of money. Two weeks later, I met with my boss at my 9-to-5. With sweaty palms, I told my boss how much I appreciated my time working at the company, but I had an opportunity to pursue a full-time career doing something I loved and I was putting in my two weeks. This was the most liberating feeling I've ever experienced in my life. The day I walked out of the office for the last time, I felt like shackles fell off my wrists and the world was alive with new opportunities. Life that had been black and white suddenly came alive in color.

By the end of that year, I made $113,643.86 running my videography business full-time. I made twice as much money as I would have working my 9-to-5, I had the ultimate freedom of being my own boss, and I finally felt like I was living the life I was meant to live. It all started with buying my first camera.

Chapter 4

YOU CAN DO IT TOO

O wning a camera is like having a superpower. It's a tool you can take with you wherever you go, and it unlocks doors to opportunities you never would have imagined. Like any great superhero, you first have to learn to master your power.

As I've navigated through my journey in videography, I've come across countless videographers who are passionate about videography but haven't built a significant business out of it because they don't know how. I have seen so many people settle for a life of working a job that they don't enjoy, making less than they want to make, and left feeling that there is a better way. I know that if these people had a roadmap to get started that they could live a life that was far more rewarding.

My goal with this book is to provide the blueprint for you to grow your videography business to a six-figure income, whether that be earning $50,000 on the side to enhance your primary income or making a full-time career out of your business, earning $100,000-plus a year. I want to equip you with the knowledge to make your financial and personal goals a reality using videography as the driver to get you there. My ultimate mission is to help one thousand videographers scale their business to six figures, enabling them to live a fuller and more rewarding life.

An Overview of What You'll Learn

In this book, I will teach you the following four steps to turn your camera into a six-figure videography business:

1. Mastering Your Mindset
2. Nailing Your Niche
3. Building Your Brand
4. The 3-Phase Approach to 6-Figure Sales

This book is built on the foundation of what worked for me, what didn't work for me, and what I learned over the process of scaling my business to six figures. My mission is to help you achieve six figures faster than I did. It took me seven years of owning a camera, but only two years of concentrated effort to accomplish this goal. I've distilled seven years of my experience into this book. Through the process I lay out, I hope to help you skip the seven-year trial-and-error period that it took me to scale my business. My mission is to help you achieve six figures in 10 to 12 months. Follow the steps laid out in this book, and you will find yourself well on your way.

The content in this book is applicable to you whether you're hoping to turn videography into a profitable side income or into a full-time career. The principles are the same. My hope is that this book speaks to you in a practical and meaningful way. This is not a book teaching the technical aspects of video production. The truth of the matter is, no matter the technical skills you have, it is the business skills that are going to be the driving force behind growing your business. These are the skills that you will learn in this book.

If you want to learn more about the technical skills necessary to level up your videography, go check out my YouTube channel where I release free content teaching the tools and techniques that go into mastering videography. You can find my channel at https://www.youtube.com/@GrantBurks.

I want to set the hard expectation that this book does not describe a get-rich-quick scheme. If you want a get-rich-quick scheme, there are plenty of resources on the internet that will sell you the world, turn you upside down, shake you until your pockets are empty, and disappear never to be heard from again. This journey is going to take hard work and dedication. "Nothing worth having comes easy" is a quote by Theodore Roosevelt that I fully believe in.

This path requires consistent, deliberate, hard work. The good news is that the work is laid out for you in these pages. The challenge is choosing to make positive progress every single day. Look at this process like building a brick house.

The work is simple, but every day you need to show up and lay another brick. Once you're finished, you're going to have built something that will change your life. A business that can provide you financial freedom, personal freedom, and a fulfilling career.

For those that want to accomplish their goals faster and easier, my hope is that this book is the first step in that process. For those that know they can make this dream a reality but want even more focused attention and support along the way, I have created an online coaching program called Videography University.

As was briefly mentioned at the start of Section 1, Videography University is an online coaching program where we provide one-on-one coaching to help you in any areas where you need assistance as you grow your business. As a member, you get access to our Private Facebook Group with other students where you can ask questions about any challenges you are facing, and you can access additional training videos breaking down the technical side of videography/ video production. I created Videography University to provide you personal coaching and accountability to help you achieve your goals of turning your videography business into a six-figure income.

If you are serious about growing your business and want support along the way, then book a free call with my team to see if Videography University is a good fit. If it seems a good fit for all parties, we'll talk about next steps for helping you achieve the six-figure mark with your videography business. To book a free call with one of our coaches, go to www.videography-university.com/apply.

Now, like all things built to last, it starts with a strong foundation.

Action Time:

At the end of at least one chapter in each section, I'll include an "Action Time" section. This section will provide you guidance on your immediate next steps along with links to any helpful resources. Remember, knowledge without action is useless. Complete the action steps at the end of the chapters, and you will see your business move in the right direction. Here is the Action Time for the first section:

1. Go to www.videography-university.com/course to gain your free login for access to the companion course for this book. Within the video modules of this course, I break down the concepts taught in this book and provide accompanying documents to help you get more value along the way. Many of the resources found in the Action Time sections can be downloaded from within this course.

2. If you know you want to grow your videography business faster and would like more hands-on guidance and help, book a call with me and my Videography University team at www.videography-university.com/apply.

Section 2

Mastering Your Mindset

Chapter 5

FIND YOUR "WHY"

When I bought my first camera and started shooting videos, everything was easy. I was in college, I had few responsibilities, I owned a camera, and it was just fun. The fact that I was making a few hundred dollars to shoot projects was icing on the cake. I saw it as a way to make some cash doing something I loved. I thought there could be a route to doing this full-time in the future, but I didn't yet know what that looked like, and I wasn't worried about figuring it out at the time. I was a college kid taking life one day at a time. No plan, no vision. That left me unprepared to make a full-time career with videography out of college.

Once doubts crept in, I leaned on words from the nay-sayers. I didn't have a vision, I didn't have a "why." I hadn't built a support system that would help lift me up and right my path when things got tough. For this reason, my journey to building the life I wanted took longer than it could have. When that college kid felt like there was no future in running a videography business, he pushed his dreams to the side and chose a path that, from the critic's perspective, was safer and more secure.

I got a job, I worked a 9-to-5, and I was left empty and desiring something more in life. I don't want you to be that version of me. The person who sidelined their dreams for a 9-to-5 that left them wanting more out of life. I want to save you from the years of frustration. It all starts with a vision and finding your "why." Your vision and your "why" serve as the North Star that will keep you on track when doubts fill your mind.

What's your "why"? Your "why" is the reason why you are setting out on your journey. Your "why" is what will keep you going when times get tough. Your "why" can be identified by answering the following three questions:

1. What is the impact you want this videography business to have on your life?
2. Who are you pursuing this dream for?
3. What is the greater impact you would like to have through pursuing this dream?

Question 1: What is the impact you want this videography business to have on your life?

That is a big question and might feel overwhelming, but let's break it down even further. To start, what financial impact do you want your videography business to have on your life?

Personally, I hated the idea of a company putting a cap on my potential with a salary. For some people, having a set yearly income works for them. Kevin O'Leary, a billionaire entrepreneur and personality on the popular show *Shark Tank*, says, "A salary is the bribe they give you to give up on your dreams." Many people opt for the "security" of a salary over pursuing their dreams and aspirations in life. As I said, some people prefer the format of a consistent paycheck. They want to know that the same amount of money will be hitting their bank account regularly.

As someone who wanted to work harder to make more, I hated that concept. I wanted to work hard and reap the rewards of my efforts. I didn't want my potential to be capped. I wanted to grow a business and see my income grow in response.

A financial goal of mine was being able to "retire" at an early age. By "retire," I mean being able to do the work I want because I want to, not because I have to. I wanted to earn the kind of money that would allow me to save, invest, and spend my life working on my own terms. The thought of working a job I hated from 9-to-5 every day for 30-plus years so that I could afford retirement did not sit well with me. I had a mission of earning six figures per year doing what I loved by the time I was 30.

Another financial goal of mine was to build a business that I could sell some day. When working for a company, you're helping to grow somebody else's business, all while money is being made off of your back. The main function of an employee is that they earn the business more than they cost the business, which allows the business to make money and grow. There's nothing wrong with this system as this structure works really well for the vast majority of the population. At the same time, this did not work well for me. I wanted to work hard to grow my own business so that someday I could sell it and receive the financial rewards of the business I built.

Outside of financial benefits, think about how this business can impact your entire lifestyle. When I worked my corporate job, I felt trapped. I worked for a company that went to great lengths to provide their employees with quality benefits, work flexibility, and a positive work-life balance, but I still felt trapped.

I felt like I had to get back to my team members immediately with answers to questions, I felt like I had to be available to my boss at all times, and I absolutely hated having to ask permission to take a day off of work. It's possible that many others don't experience the same sentiment working a 9-to-5, but it was unshakeable for me. I felt like the focus was not "Am I helping build a better business?" and instead was "Do people here like me?"

I dreamed of being able to do the work I needed to do that allowed me to take the time away that I wanted to. I dreamed of a world where I did not have to ask permission from anyone to take time away. If I wanted to take a day off, I shut down my computer and took a day off. No permission needed and no fear of colleagues asking where I was.

Ask yourself that same question, "What is the impact I want this to have on my life?" Maybe your answers are the same as mine, or maybe they are different. Is there a dream purchase you want to be able to afford some day? Is the flexibility of being your own boss something that motivates you? For now, just think about those questions.

Question 2: Who are you pursuing this dream for?

For many people, a career change will impact others in their life. For me, I was married at the time that I made the leap to going full-time with my videography business. My wife and I also hoped to have kids in the near future. I made this goal of pursuing this business full-time for my wife and our future kids. I wanted my wife to be free to chase her own dreams in life without the pressure of feeling like she had to work a certain job to help provide for our family. I wanted to be able to financially provide an amazing life for our future children.

I had dreams of being able to help them pursue their own dreams, provide a lifestyle that would allow us to make amazing memories on trips together, and build a business that would inspire them and show them that they can build the life they dream of if they stay persistent and work hard. Who is it that you are pursuing this dream for?

Maybe it's just you. That's not a bad thing by any means. Building the life that you dream of is something that everybody should strive for. Maybe you have a significant other, a child, a relative, or a friend that you are also pursuing this career for. Maybe you're helping someone else financially, or maybe you just want to help inspire others. Whatever the case may be, ask yourself, "Who am I pursuing this for?" This takes us to our third and final question.

Question 3: What is the greater impact you would like to have through pursuing this dream?"

For me, I dreamed of earning a living that allowed me to give generously to others. There are a lot of things that I am passionate about, and I dreamed of being in a position to give to organizations that are doing positive work in the world. Another dream of mine is to be an example to anybody else that has a passion for building a business.

This is a driving force behind why I am also writing this book. Society has conditioned many of us to think that the only way to make a living is to go to college, earn a degree, get a job, and work a 30-year career in a 9-to-5. I had a lot of successful people in my life, but I did not have an immediate example of someone who took a similar career path in starting their own videography business. If I had, I think that my journey to where I am could have come more quickly. I want to be this example to others. I want people to see that not only is it possible, but starting your own business can lead you to the life of your dreams.

What kind of larger impact do you hope to have by building your videography business?

It's time to identify your "why." You can use a blank piece of paper or go to Chapter 5 of the free companion course (access the free companion course at www.videography-university.com/course) and print out our Why Document from the Film To Freedom accompanying course. If you are using our document, we have all of the questions typed out for you. If you are using a blank piece of paper, write down the following three questions:

1. What is the impact you want this videography business to have on your life?
2. Who are you pursuing this dream for?
3. What is the greater impact you would like to have through pursuing this dream?

Set a timer for 15 minutes, and write down as many thoughts as you possibly can for the answer to the first question. Recognize that I said "thoughts." The goal here is to simply get down as many ideas as you can for the first question. It's okay if they are half-baked ideas. The goal is to keep your pen moving. We'll refine the ideas later.

Next, I want you to move to the second question. Put 15 minutes back on the clock, and write out all of your ideas. You'll then follow the same process for the third question. Now, I want you to put 15 minutes back on the clock, go back to Question 1 and turn your bullets into your top three items. You will then do that same thing for the second and third questions. It's okay if you have fewer than three items for any of the questions. You just don't want there to be more than three.

Now that you have your thoughts for the three questions, it's time to consolidate these into a document that will serve as your "why" any time you have hit a roadblock or are starting to get discouraged on your journey. You will use the second page of the Why Document for this part.

After the text that reads, "I will build my videography business so that ...," write out your response to the first question. For example, mine reads, "I will build my videography business so that I can financially afford to provide for my family, have the autonomy to control my own schedule, and work hard to have financial freedom at an early age."

Then move to the next section that reads, "I am pursuing this dream for ..." and write your response to Question 2. For example, mine reads, "I am pursuing this dream for myself, my wife, and our future children."

From there, you will move to the third section that reads, "By building my videography business, I will ..." You will then write in your answer to Question 3. For example, mine reads, "By building my videography business, I will be able to give generously to charitable organizations and show my future children that they can accomplish their dreams through hard work and persistence."

There is now only one step left in the process. At the bottom of the document, you will see a section that reads, "This document serves as my 'why.' These are the reasons I am pursuing my dream of creating my own videography business. When times get tough, I will refer back to this document to remind myself why I'm working toward this goal.

Through hard work and persistence, I will achieve my goal and fulfill my 'why.'"

On the line below that, you will see a blank line. That line is waiting for your signature. This is a contract to yourself. A signed agreement serving as a constant reminder "why" you are pursuing this dream. Don't sign this contract lightly. When you sign this document, you are making a commitment to yourself. You are making a promise that you are going to do the work it takes to achieve life-changing goals.

Anytime you hear critics chirping in your ear, refer back to this document. Anytime self-doubt overtakes your self-confidence, refer back to this document. Anytime it feels as if the next step is too difficult, refer back to this document. You have a "why," and the only route to achieving that "why" is never giving up. Author Paulo Coelho writes, "The secret of life, though, is to fall seven times and to get up eight times."[1] There will be moments of difficulty, there will be mistakes made, but if you never give up, you will achieve your goal, and you will live the life you were meant to live.

Once your document is filled out, I want you to put it in a special place where you will see it often. You can frame it and hang it on your wall. You can tape it to your mirror. You can even take a picture of it and save it as the background of your phone. Put it somewhere it won't be lost and somewhere that you are forced to constantly refer back to it. Now that you've written out your "why," it's time to build your network of support.

Success isn't built in a vacuum. You will need help along the way. The best way to ensure successful follow-through is by having a source of accountability. In the next chapter, we'll talk about finding an accountability partner.

Action Time:

1. Download the Why Document in Chapter 5 of the companion course. Access the free companion course at:

   www.videography-university.com/course

2. Fill out this document, sign it, and date it. This contract to yourself will serve as a reminder as to why you are pursuing the dream of creating your own videography business.

Chapter 6

LOCK IN AN ACCOUNTABILITY PARTNER

You're the driving force behind the success of your videography business, but you're going to need support along the way. According to a study conducted by The Association for Talent Development, you are 95% more likely to accomplish a goal when you have an accountability partner that you meet with regularly to check on progress for your goals.[2] Let's look at a hypothetical scenario.

Let's say you're setting a fitness goal for yourself of losing five pounds in 30 days. Let's say you decide to go to the gym every day by yourself and track what you eat on your own. Now let's say you have the same goal, but instead you go to the gym every day with someone else who is also trying to lose weight. In addition, you and your friend track meals together to ensure you're hitting your calorie goals.

I know, personally, I would be far more likely to achieve the goal if I were to take the second route, by going on the journey with a friend. There's a reason even athletes have trainers and nutritionists. Most athletes know every workout in the book and every nutrient they are supposed to put in their body, but the accountability of a trainer is critical to their success. Half the battle is the knowledge; the other half is the application. You're far more likely to execute when you have an accountability partner.

Let me ask you another question—have you ever purchased an online course that is purely self-paced with no additional coaching, and you find that you don't end up finishing the entire course or following through on the teachings? It is because it is hard to keep ourselves accountable when we are on an island. As social creatures, we are built to work together to accomplish our goals.

Running your own videography business can be an isolating experience; trust me, I was there. An accountability partner will remove you from your silo and help you achieve your goals along the way. You might be thinking, "But, Grant, I don't know anybody else who is trying to start their own videography business." That's okay. Neither did I! But I did have a friend who was building his business as a real estate agent. His name is Ryan Willis.

You don't have to find somebody who is on the exact same journey as you; you simply need to find somebody who is on a journey. In certain areas, it can be even more beneficial to have an accountability partner who is in a different industry. People in the same industry can see problems from the same lens and in turn attack them with the same strategies.

Somebody in a different industry can provide new ideas and a fresh perspective for ways to overcome challenges.

My first year in corporate videography, I was struggling to find new clients. I had a website and did some marketing on social media, but I struggled to connect with prospects. I shared this with my friend Ryan who, at the time, was starting his real estate business.

He said, "It sounds like you're not meeting your ideal clients where they are." I didn't understand what he meant. "Who's your ideal client?" he asked.

"Small- to medium-sized business owners," I responded.

"Well, you need to find out where those people are spending their time, and market your services there."

The light bulb went off. I spoke with a few past clients and discovered that most of my clients were either working in their business or networking in-person to grow their business. That conversation with Ryan completely changed the trajectory of my business. I began going directly to businesses offering a free video to demonstrate my work to business owners.

I additionally joined local business networking groups that were designed to help businesses lock in referrals across networks. My business grew at an alarming rate. This strategy set me apart from my competitors, and it originated as advice from my accountability partner who was in a completely different industry.

Look in your immediate network and think about who of your friends, family members, or acquaintances is on a journey of their own. It could be somebody else who has, or is starting, their own business. If you don't have anybody in your immediate network that is starting a business, get creative. It could be someone who is on a personal journey such as health and wellness. Maybe it's someone who is working toward a degree or a financial goal. Simply find somebody who is working toward a goal, and ask them if you could help keep each other accountable.

Look for somebody with the following three characteristics:

1. Someone Who Is a Good Listener
2. Someone Who Is Encouraging
3. Someone Who Is Reliable

Characteristic 1: Someone Who Is a Good Listener

When I started in videography, I was a fish out of water in regards to editing. I used Adobe Premiere Pro, and the edits I wanted to make meant hours googling keywords to figure out how to accomplish my goal. A painful number of hours were spent sifting through Adobe Forums and Quora for answers to my questions. At the time, I had a friend who was a few years ahead of me in the world of editing. Let's call him Joe. Joe told me to reach out to him anytime I needed help. When I would get to the point of hopelessness, I would give Joe a call, but it was always the same old song and dance.

Instead of finding the answer to my question, I would end up talking about whatever was happening in Joe's life for an hour just to end the call where I began except with one less hour left in my day. Joe was a nice guy, but he always managed to steer the conversation back toward himself. Most of us have that type of person in our lives. At the other end of the spectrum, I had another friend in Kyler Holland who was always willing and available to answer my questions. Find a Kyler, not a Joe.

With that being said, don't be a Joe either. You need to provide equal value to your accountability partner. That is the key to creating long-lasting relationships that will help you grow and scale your business.

Characteristic 2: Someone Who Is Encouraging

An encouraging attitude is a critical component of a quality accountability partner. There are more than enough critics and naysayers out in the world. They are bound to fill your network as well. When times get tough and challenges arise, you need to be able to lean on your accountability partner for encouragement. Few things can be quite as damaging as being met with negativity when you are looking for support from someone.

Look for someone who will be a source of optimism when you are feeling discouraged. Someone who will pick you up when you are feeling down. Don't fall into the trap of leaning on somebody who is just going to tell you whatever you want to hear. You need somebody who will be willing to provide you with good advice, but there's a difference between being honest and being a pessimist. Honest optimists make the best accountability partners.

Characteristic 3: Someone Who Is Reliable

Lastly, it's important that you find someone who is reliable. Have you ever needed an answer to a question, so you reached out to someone just to receive radio silence on the other end? You need to know that your accountability partner is going to be there when you need them. Don't expect them to be sitting by their phone 24/7, spending their days waiting on you hand and foot, but your accountability partner should prioritize getting back to you as soon as they are able to. It shouldn't take you days to get an answer from them. They should understand and respect how important they are to the growth of your business.

This goes for you as well. Prioritize being responsive in your communication to your accountability partner. Don't ignore their messages when they need something. That's how you can sour a great working relationship. It sounds simple on the surface, but it's easy to let a message go unanswered for a few hours. A few hours turns into a day, and then you forget to respond at all. All of a sudden it becomes a habit, and that relationship deteriorates. Prioritize your accountability partner, and they will be one of the biggest assets to the success of your videography business.

Now that we've reviewed the characteristics of a good accountability partner, I've got some great news: You don't have to limit yourself to a single accountability partner. Try to find multiple. You might have one friend that you lean on most or have the best relationship with, but it's good to have a handful of people you can consistently rely on for support. I personally have around five accountability partners between my friends and family.

How do you go about finding an accountability partner? Navigate to Chapter 6 of the free Film to Freedom companion course (you can access this free course at www.videography-university.com/course), and print off the Accountability Partner Document. You can also use a blank sheet of paper if you'd prefer.

Set a timer for 15 minutes, and list out all of your closest friends. If you notice yourself hitting a stalling point, open your phone, and go to your text messages. Scroll through the most recent names that populate your list of text messages. Another great place to look is social media. Go to your social media pages, and click on your DMs. Take note of the most recent names of people you have messaged. Keep writing for 15 minutes. Try to put together a list of 15 or more people.

With the three characteristics of an effective accountability partner in mind—a good listener, encouraging, and reliable—go through and circle each person that can be characterized by all three of the qualities. Be critical. Your goal should be to end up with four to seven names.

Once you have your list of four to seven people, you have your core list of accountability partners. Shoot them each a message providing them two statements and one question:

1. Statement: what you're doing
2. Statement: what they mean to you
3. Question: if they are on a journey too, could you both keep each other accountable?

For example, if I were going to message someone I was interested in partnering with as an accountability partner, my message would look something like this:

> *Hey Ryan! I was just thinking about you and our friendship. You've always been somebody that I have looked up to in life. You're reliable, hard-working, and thoughtful. I'm working on building a career in videography. As I work to start up my business, I know I'm going to hit bumps along the way, and frankly it feels a little bit daunting. I would love to have an accountability partner to bounce ideas off of/be able to get encouragement from when I hit roadblocks. You came up as someone who would make for a great accountability partner!*
>
> *I also thought it would be great if there was a journey that you're going on that I could help keep you accountable on as well. It will help us accomplish our goals together! Would you be willing to be my accountability partner, and is there something I can be your accountability partner for as well?*

Feel free to craft your message in your own words, or copy and paste the one above. Then hit the almighty "send" button. It might feel daunting at first, but you're accomplishing a few different things by hitting "send."

1. *You're empowering yourself.*

This might be the first time you're sharing this dream of yours with someone else. Sharing your dreams and ambitions is scary. What if someone laughs at them? Some people are born with confidence, and some have to acquire it over time. I was not one of the lucky few who was born with confidence.

Over time, I realized something: If I wanted to make the most out of this life I am given, I had to forget what critics thought of me. That realization allowed me to have some of the best experiences of my life. I never would have tried out to be a college mascot if I was afraid people might laugh at me if I didn't make the team. I never would have started my videography business if I cared if people thought I was foolish for chasing my dreams. I never would have written this book if I was too afraid that people would criticize me.

If I was too afraid of what people thought to do any of those things, I never would have had the chance to run out onto a football field surrounded by 110,000 people, I never would have chased the dream that has allowed me to have complete control over my life and provide a better financial future for my family, and I never would have been able to help you accomplish your dreams with your business.

I didn't try out to be Ohio State's mascot for those who would laugh at me if I failed; I tried out for me. I didn't build a videography business for people who said it wasn't possible; I did it for my family. And I didn't write this book for people who said I had no value to provide; I wrote it for you.

Every time I turn on my phone, I'm met with the quote, "There is only one way to avoid criticism: do nothing, say nothing, be nothing." When I read this quote, it reminds me of an important message. I googled it the first time I read it to see if I could find out where it originated. Some sources say it is from Aristotle, and some say it is from a 19th century writer named Elbert Hubbard.

Whether it was written 100 or 2,000 years ago, critics have been around for all of humanity, and they're not going anywhere in the future. It is the Aristotles and Elbert Hubbards who are able to overcome the judgment of others that go on to live their fullest lives and change countless lives in the process. How do we build confidence? Through small actions.

Little by little, take action that requires confidence, and, over time, you will find your confidence has grown. It's like making deposits into a bank account. Each time you flex this muscle, you become a little bit more comfortable until, over time, you find what once felt impossible now becomes second nature. When you hit that "send" button to your accountability partner, you're taking one small step toward building your confidence and empowering yourself to build your business.

2. You're creating a strong foundation.

The second thing you're doing is building your support system by using the right material. You may be familiar with "The Parable of the Two Builders." In this parable, we have two different people undertaking the same task: building a house. For the first person, he builds his house on sturdy material: rock. The second man builds his house on unstable terrain: sand. It's only the man who builds his house on the strong foundation who builds a structure that withstands all of the challenges life throws his way.

When you hit that "send" button, you are building your business on rock. You are bringing along reliable people that you can lean on for support when the winds blow and the floods come. If you don't hit "send," and you don't create your team of support, you risk building your business on sand. For most of us, it is much harder to forge ahead on a journey when we don't have anyone by our side when things get tough, so build your house on rock and send your accountability partners that first message.

Now that you have your team of accountability partners, you are on your way toward creating a strong business. At this point, it's time to reinforce your team of support with other resources. Now you surround yourself with the right material.

Action Time:

1. Download the Accountability Partner Document in Chapter 6 of the free Film to Freedom accompanying course (you can access the course at www.videogra-phy-university.com/course). Complete the exercise we reviewed in this chapter to identify one to four accountability partners.

2. Send a text message or call your one to four prospective accountability partners to confirm they will partner with you on your journey.

Chapter 7

FLOOD YOUR MIND WITH HELPFUL RESOURCES

You have your support team in your accountability partners, so it's time to fill your mind with as much quality content as possible. Continuously filling your mind with valuable content is the key to creating unstoppable momentum.

Along the way you will find critics lining up, filling your ear with whispers of why your dreams are impossible. The truth is, most of these critics want to whisper doubts in your ear because they abandoned their dreams long ago. As human beings, we tend to become what we surround ourselves with. Jack Canfield, the famed author of the *Chicken Soup for the Soul* series, once wrote, "You are the average of the five people you spend the most time with."[3]

The more time you spend around a group of people, the more you are inclined to speak like them, act like them, and be like them. After spending an extended period of time around someone, have you ever noticed yourself using phrases they use, words they use, or mannerisms they use?

While I believe this quote holds weight, I believe it would be more accurately stated, "Your life becomes an average of the content you fill your mind with." This includes the people we surround ourselves with, but it does not stop there. This also includes what we read, what we listen to, and what we spend our time watching. For this reason, it's important that you surround yourself with positivity from credible sources. People who have accomplished what you are striving to achieve.

Unfortunately, not all of us have an immediate relationship with someone who has created their own successful videography business. I know I sure didn't. Fear not, you will see in this chapter that you have access to all of the resources you need to surround yourself with the encouragement and external accountability you need to build your videography business. It's a simple fact that challenges will present themselves along the journey, but this section will equip you with the tools you need to break through those barriers and ultimately achieve the life you were made to live. It's time to flood your mind with helpful tools and resources.

In this phase, you're going to identify resources that will motivate, educate, and inspire you as you continue on your journey of starting your videography business. The end goal of any of these outlets is to encourage you to push forward when obstacles arise. The key is to find content that you enjoy consuming that also inspires you to accomplish your next goal. As you work toward your goals and consume this content all the while, you will create unstoppable momentum.

You will begin to see the world through the lens of the "owner and operator of a six-figure videography business." You will be learning and growing at all times throughout the day. This process changed my business in my second year doing videography part-time.

In 2019, I created my LLC. That was the year I began treating videography like a business instead of a hobby. At the time, I was working a corporate job, so I dedicated my weeknights and weekends towards shooting and editing. Creating an LLC lit a fire inside of me, and all hours of every day I wanted to learn more about my craft. Physical exercise has always been an important part of my life. I thought to myself, "I spend an hour almost every day working out. What if I could find a way to kill two birds with one stone and hone my craft of videography while I work out?"

I did a quick Google search for "videography," and I saw a number of hits pop up for YouTube videos. I found a wealth of knowledge on YouTube. Channels such as Peter McKinnon, Matti Haapoja, Danny Gevirtz, Epic Light Media, Potato Jet, Matt WhoisMatt Johnson, Gerald Undone, and the list goes on.

I started consuming content from these channels any opportunity that I had. I listened to videos while I was driving, while I worked out, while I cooked, and suddenly, I noticed that I was improving my craft and growing my business from tips I picked up from these videos. Many of these were ideas I probably never would have thought of on my own, but because I flooded my mind with quality content about videography, I was able to level up my business. I was like a sponge, soaking up knowledge throughout all hours of every day.

I want you to identify three online resources that you can use to flood your mind with videography-related content. How can you identify three sources of content that will help you to learn, grow, and stay motivated as you build your videography business? Go to Chapter 7 of the free Film to Freecom accompanying course (you can access this course for free by going to www.videography-university.com/course) to access a list of resources that I found insightful and motivational as I worked to scale my videography business. On this free list, we have compiled podcasts, YouTube channels, websites, and more items that are chock full of valuable videography-related information.

You can also do a search for "videography" on Spotify, YouTube, and Google to find other resources that you might enjoy learning from. Lean on these resources, tune in whenever you're able, and watch as you grow in your skill and business.

Now that you are filling your mind with resources that will help you level up your videography skills, the next step is identifying your niche.

Action Time:

1. Go to Chapter 7 of the free Film to Freecom accompanying course (you can access this course for free by going to www.videography-university.com/course) to access our list of preferred videography podcasts, YouTube channels, and websites that you can learn from as you work to build your business.

2. Select three to four resources and bookmark them so that you can easily access them and fill your mind with their valuable information throughout your day.

Section 3

Nailing Your Niche

Chapter 8

The Riches Are in the Niches

You have a strong foundation of support for yourself, and now you might be wondering, "How do I get clients?" We will talk more about how to find and secure clients in Section 5: The 3-Phase Approach to 6-Figure Sales. Before you can focus on the strategies to secure clients, you have to ask yourself another question: "What type of client do I want to serve?" You have a decision to make—is your business going to be a shotgun or a rifle? What do I mean?

A shotgun fires small pellets known as "shot." Hence the name "shotgun." These pellets fan out, casting a wide net. The shotgun is known for its ability to hit a target within a large radius, not for its accuracy. Shotguns are great for hunting small game, like birds.

A rifle fires a single projectile known as a bullet. With its rifled barrel, a rifle sends the singular projectile farther on a more accurate path. You can hit your designated target in your intended area from a farther distance with a rifle. Rifles are known for their accuracy at long ranges. A rifle is intended for hunting large game, such as deer, elk, and even bears.

With the shotgun approach, you are casting a wide net to seek out business anywhere and everywhere. This is often referred to in the videography world as being a generalist. With the rifle approach, you are seeking out targeted clients that fall within a specific niche. This is referred to as serving a niche. In this chapter, we are going to discuss the advantages and disadvantages to being a generalist versus serving a niche. To start, let's talk about why they say the riches are in the niches.

You may have heard the phrase before, "The riches are in the niches." What does this mean? It means that your videography business is going to be more profitable by niching down and serving a targeted demographic of clients. When we look back at the shotgun versus rifle approach, we see that the shotgun is best for hunting small game while the rifle is the key to landing large game.

You might be thinking, "But a lot of smaller clients can add up to the same amount of revenue as one large client." You are correct! It's possible to land a lot of smaller clients and create a business model off of this structure. Even in this business model, success is most likely to be found by serving a lot of smaller clients within the same niche. We'll talk more about this later in the chapter, but for now, let's look at three reasons you should greatly consider serving a niche:

1. You can charge a premium for your services.
2. You save on operating costs.
3. You have an easier time finding clients.

Let's first take a look at how serving a niche enables you to charge a premium for your services.

How does serving a niche allow you to charge a premium for your services?

We don't have to look far to see this concept play out on a large scale. By 1971, there was a fast-food restaurant on every corner offering a warm cup of coffee, but three men saw an opportunity to provide customers with a unique product that would differentiate their coffee from the standard cup of Joe.[3] In 1971, Jerry Baldwin, Zev Siegl, and Gordon Bowker started a company by the name of Starbucks. At the onset, Starbucks was not much different than any other local coffee shop, but in 1982, the company hired a man by the name of Howard Schultz to manage the company's retail sales and marketing. Schultz visited Milan to study the Italian city's renowned coffee culture.

Upon his return, Schultz had a new vision for the small company. He wanted to build a coffee shop that focused on fostering connection, having conversations, and one that created a sense of community. The founders had different plans in mind, so the two parties agreed to part ways. Schultz took his vision and put it into action with a different coffee shop. Schultz's company took off. Schultz returned to his previous colleagues who were experiencing challenges with their Starbucks locations and provided them an offer to purchase the chain of six stores. The owners agreed to the sale price, and Starbucks was now under the leadership of Howard Schulz.

As the newfound owner, Schultz quickly implemented his original vision for Starbucks, to provide its customers with a superior coffee-buying experience. What was previously a quick cup of coffee from McDonalds to start your day turned into a warm, welcoming "Good morning!" from your Starbucks barista who knew you by name. A trip to Starbucks was more than a transaction; it was an experience.

At McDonalds, you could get a quick burger, chicken sandwich, french fries, McFlurry, a Happy Meal for your kid, a salad for health-conscious consumers, or one of the many other items on their menu. You could also get a cup of coffee.

At Starbucks, you could expect a premium cup of coffee accompanied by a premium customer experience at a premium price. Starbucks was able to infiltrate the market that other companies already served because they provided a specialized product and experience. When people went to McDonalds, they knew coffee was on the menu. When they went to Starbucks, coffee *was* the menu. Starbucks niched down and said, 'We are going to offer customers coffee, and we are going to offer them the best cup of coffee we can!' This specialization by Starbucks allowed them to charge a premium price for their product. Starbucks took the rifle approach.

When you go to a restaurant and you see a never-ending list of items on the menu, what do you think?

"Jack of all trades, master of none."

Inversely, when you go to a restaurant and the menu is a select number of specialized items, what do you think?

"Best _____ in town!"

Starbucks limited their menu, so they could be the "best coffee in town!" Today, a medium cup of black coffee from McDonalds costs $1.69. A medium cup of plain black coffee from Starbucks costs $2.99. That is almost twice the cost of McDonalds'. An increase of $1.30 over four billion cups of coffee per year provides for a nice healthy bottom line. Don't be a jack of all trades; be a master of *one*!

Put yourself in the shoes of Starbucks as it relates to videography. Imagine charging twice what your competitors charge, yet your inbox remains filled with new inquiries every day. That sounds like a pretty good place to be, doesn't it? That is the power of specializing in a niche. As they say, the riches are in the niches. The benefits to the bottom line of your business don't stop there. Not only are you going to be able to charge more money by niching down, you will also save more money.

How does serving a niche help you save money?

In business, you can think of your gross profit as the money that ends up in your pocket. For simplicity's sake, think of this as your revenue minus your operating expenses. This means there are two main ways to increase the money you keep: either increasing revenue or decreasing expenses. As outlined in the Starbucks example, specializing in a niche enables you to increase revenue by charging premium prices. Niching down has the added benefit of decreasing operating expenses.

Let's review two different business models: a videography business that specializes in producing corporate brand videos for small- to medium-sized businesses and a videography business that does anything and everything. First, let's look at Scenario 1. For a videography business that specializes in producing corporate brand videos for small- to medium-sized businesses, you will likely be investing in gear that allows you to capture interviews of employees, as well as B-roll of the daily operations of a company.

For both of these items you will need a camera, a lighting kit, an audio kit, and a stabilizer of some sort. Of course, there are additional items you could purchase, but you could get away with that package for a basic setup. For editing, you'll want an editing program of some sort, such as Adobe Premiere Pro or Davinci Resolve.

Now, let's consider the scenario of a generalist videography business. A generalist videography business would be serving a wide variety of clients with a wide variety of deliverables. Some of the videos they could produce for clients include corporate website videos, corporate social media videos, wedding videography, real estate videography, sport/fitness videography, product videography, animated videos, and the list goes on.

Maybe you don't even limit your company to videography, maybe you offer photography as well. Now you could receive inquiries for corporate headshots, wedding photography, corporate event photography, family portraits, and much more. With this company structure, you're going to need multiple cameras, numerous lenses, lighting kits, flashes, strobes, a drone, access to a studio, software for editing videos, software for editing photos, but it doesn't stop there. You will need software to send deliverables to your respective clients, and you will likely want to utilize a platform that is targeted toward your end client. You probably won't use the same platform to deliver corporate website videos that you would to deliver a digital album of wedding photos to a couple.

As you can see, the production costs increase dramatically with the generalist approach. Even more important than the difference in operational expenses is the difference in time spent learning new skills. As owner and operator of a videography business, time is your biggest asset as well as your most limited resource. Time is something that we have a finite amount of. It's always possible to earn more money, and as you build your business, you will see that money can come easier than you ever thought, but time is something that you can never get more of. We all have the same 24 hours a day, so it's important that you use them wisely.

When you niche your business, you are going to spend all of your time focused on a single industry or single type of video. Through this singular focus, you will become an expert in your niche. Think about it like this, if you were a lumberjack and spent every day cutting down trees, you would quickly learn the perfect angle, velocity, and pattern to cut down a tree in the most efficient manner. When someone chooses to be a generalist, they spread their time between a variety of industries. This makes it difficult to master any one industry. Most likely you will end up as a jack of all trades and master of none. It will take you longer to provide an inferior product than someone who has specialized in a niche. Most clients don't want to hire a jack of all trades for their project; they want to hire the master.

Let's look back at the lumberjack example. Let's say instead of specializing as a lumberjack, you own a generalist landscaping company. Your week consists of cutting down trees, mulching flower beds, planting flowers, mowing lawns, trimming hedges, and cleaning gutters. You are now dividing your time amongst a variety of tasks. It will take you far longer to master any one of these skills, which means that you will take longer to accomplish each of them individually. The opportunity cost of taking longer on each individual task is a loss in potential profits. The extra time you're spending accomplishing each separate task is time that could be spent focusing on landing more clients. On the topic of landing more clients, niching down will save you time in trying to locate new clients.

How does having a niche make it easier to find prospective clients?

Landing clients is often a challenge, if not the most challenging task, for any business. A large amount of time and effort is spent tracking down prospects, figuring out if these prospects are a good fit for your services, building trust with the clients, and ultimately landing them as a paid client. The moment many businesses go wrong is when they try to serve everybody. It might seem counterintuitive, but there is a popular saying in marketing, "If you try to serve everybody, you will serve nobody." Let's take a deeper dive into this concept.

As a generalist, where do you start with your marketing? Should you reach out to small business owners interested in website video content? Should you connect with real estate agents interested in real estate videography? Should you reach out to newly engaged couples looking for a wedding videographer? What happens when you connect with any of these individuals and they go to your website? They are going to see a hodgepodge of video work. A corporate video, a wedding video, a real estate video, a music video—what will they think when they see this?

"This videographer doesn't specialize in what we need."

The prospective client will continue their search elsewhere for a videographer who specializes in the kind of video they are looking for. This becomes a long, drawn-out process of trying to build your client base. Once you do find a client that is interested in your services, they are likely interested in your services for all the wrong reasons. They probably think that your prices will be cheaper than your competitors. As we discussed earlier, when people go to McDonalds, they expect McDonalds prices. When people go to Starbucks, they expect to pay a premium price for a premium product. If a client sees videos serving a multitude of industries for a multitude of purposes, they are going to see McDonalds: a large menu and cheap prices.

You make it far easier to prospect when you specialize in a niche. More on prospecting in Section 5, but for now, know the first step to finding new clients is to know your target client. As a generalist, you have no target client. Your target client is anybody and everybody. As a specialist, you have a built-in target client. Your target client is the decision maker for the niche you are specializing in.

If you specialize in real estate videography, your target client is real estate agents. If you specialize in wedding videography, your target client is newly engaged couples. If you specialize in brand videos for dental practices, your target client is dental practice owners. If you specialize in corporate videos for small- to medium-sized businesses, your target client is marketing directors or owners of small- to medium-sized businesses.

Once you know your target client, it's easier to reach them. Real estate agents will be at real estate brokerages. You can mail fliers for your services to every real estate brokerage in your area.

Newly engaged couples will be joining local Facebook groups for wedding dresses, venues, and other wedding day inspiration. You can join these groups, message couples congratulating them on their engagement, and offer your services as a wedding videographer.

Owners of dental practices will be listed on their websites. You can search "dental practices near me" in Google, and this will pull up all of the dental practices in your area. From there, use a website like Hunter.io to scan the website for emails of people at the practice. Once you locate an email, send them a message offering your services. Or even better, drive to the practice, and offer a free video with the option for a paid full-length video if the practice likes the free video. More on this later!

I know these methods work because I have personally done all of them, and they are what has allowed me to turn my videography business into a six-figure business. (We will review a detailed breakdown of getting sales in Section 5: The 3-Phase Approach to 6-Figure Sales.) I reached out to brokerages and gained a handful of real estate agents interested in my services. I fostered those relationships and now have a steady stream of agents that I shoot real estate listings for.

I did outreach to newly engaged couples on Facebook, and now I have a wedding videography business that runs on autopilot with leads hitting my inbox daily from couples interested in my company's wedding videography services.

My company books out a year in advance, and now we send all of our new inquiries to other local videographers.

I scoured emails from dental practice websites and offered free work with the opportunity for a full-length paid video. That process turned into tens of thousands of dollars in yearly work.

You may be thinking, "But, Grant, you said to specialize in a niche, it sounds like you serve multiple niches." The key is to start in a niche, this is how you gain a foothold, master this niche, then scale. Let's look at a well-known entrepreneur that utilized this strategy to grow his business.

Chapter 9

SCALING YOUR BUSINESS

O n July 5, 1994, a man decided to leave his Wall Street job to pursue building a company in the ecommerce space.[4] This man had a challenge on his hands—in what industry did he want to found his company? He created a list of 20 products he felt that he could market on the internet. He narrowed down that list to what he felt were the five most promising products. This list included CDs, computer hardware, computer software, videos, and books. As he reviewed this list of five products, he felt that books would be the best option due to the worldwide demand for literature, the low unit price for books, and the large catalog of books that were available for print. This was the inception of Amazon.com: Jeff Bezos's vision to create the world's largest online bookstore.

It's important to highlight that Bezos did not try creating his company on the principle of being the world's largest online retailer of everything. Bezos chose a single product to sell: books. He chose a single niche to dominate. By selecting a niche to specialize in, he was able to master that niche. His company became the world's top online retailer of books because selling books online was all they did. What did Bezos do once he mastered his niche? He expanded into other markets.

In 1998, Amazon extended their offering outside of books to offer ecommerce for CDs. The company used the principles that they learned from dominating the online book sale industry to expand into selling CDs online. A year later, they expanded into additional categories such as toys, electronics, and tools. The key to this future growth was Amazon's plan to start niched. Today, Amazon does everything from ecommerce to cloud computing to digital streaming to ventures into artificial intelligence. This all started with an online bookstore.

It begs the question, "Would Bezos ever have been able to build the company he has built if he tried to serve all of these markets at the onset? Would he have amassed his $121.8 billion net worth if he tried to be a jack of all trades right out of the gate?" It's impossible to say, but I have a feeling that the answer is no. Without mastering an industry before moving to the next, his company probably would not have succeeded in the way that it has. The Amazon model is the model for how I have grown my business and how I recommend you grow yours.

I started as a wedding videographer. Once I gained a strong foothold in this niche and created systems that allowed me to put it on autopilot, I expanded into producing brand videos for small- to medium-sized businesses. Once I felt I had a strong footing in corporate brand videos, I moved into corporate social media content. Once I created systems for operating and growing the corporate side of my videography business, I expanded into real estate listings. This path has allowed me to create a sustainable business that grows with each area of the business feeding into the other.

My wedding clients bring in corporate clients, my corporate clients turn to monthly clients, and my monthly clients share my services with friends or colleagues that are real estate agents. This process works in every direction. Each area of my business feeds into the other, which results in the simultaneous growth of every area of the company. In business, this is what is called the flywheel effect.

A flywheel is a disk located inside of machines such as cars, power hammers, lawn mowers, and even rowing machines. When energy is put into a flywheel, the flywheel stores that energy providing for continued movement. Think of a rowing machine, for example. When you pull the handle of the rail, the flywheel starts to spin. You can hear the rushing of air or swishing of water depending on what type of machine you're on. As you continue rowing, it becomes easier to maintain pace. This is because the flywheel has stored up kinetic energy. If you were to stop, the machine would not turn off like a light. It would slowly spin to a stop over time. A business can function in the same manner.

If you grow your business, parts of your business can feed into other parts of your business, providing continuous growth. Your initial set up and operation of a niche acts as the source of energy to create clients for other areas of your business. Mastering that niche acts as the first pull on the handle for the rowing machine, putting your business into motion. From there, you create systems that keep your business running. Those systems act as the pulls that provide continued energy to the flywheel.

Once you expand into a new niche, the niches you have already mastered feed into your new niche. This is the stored energy from the flywheel that provides continuous life to the rest of your business. The process continues in a circular fashion, sending your business in a constant upward trajectory. The process is as follows: find your niche, master your niche, create systems, expand into a new niche, repeat the process; watch your business grow. It all starts with the first step: identify your niche. Let's talk about how to identify your niche.

Chapter 10

IDENTIFY YOUR NICHE

Now that you know the benefits of serving a niche with your videography business, it's time to identify your niche. Start by navigating to Chapter 10 of the free Film to Freedom companion course for this book (you can access this course for free by going to www.videography-university.com/course). This will take you to a list of profitable niches. From there, read through the list, and write down the five niches that sound most enjoyable to build your videography business in.

It's important that you enjoy doing work for the industry that you decide to niche in. Enjoying the work that you do will make it much easier to build a videography business that thrives in its respective niche. Don't get me wrong, it's possible to enjoy the money and success enough to overcome not loving the work, but a perfect fit is finding financial success and enjoying the process along the way.

You should now have five profitable niches that you would enjoy working in that you can choose from. From there, consider the five niches, and think about whether or not you have anybody in your network who is, or knows somebody who is, a decision maker in one of those five industries. For example, when I was looking to expand my business, I knew that real estate was an industry that interested me, and I also had a friend in my network, Ryan Willis, who was a real estate agent. I decided to pursue this niche because I felt I could get a foothold by leveraging that relationship to build a portfolio.

When you look at the list of your top five options, if you know that you have an immediate or secondary connection with someone who is a decision maker in one of those niches, I recommend starting with that niche. If you know decision makers in two of the niches, I recommend selecting the niche that you are most passionate about.

If you don't know anybody that is a decision maker in any of the niches, sell your camera and dust off your résumé. Time to find a new job. Just kidding, not a problem. I was in the same situation when I wanted to branch into shooting corporate website videos for small- to medium-sized businesses. At that point, pick whichever niche you feel most drawn to. Whatever niche you select, you are not permanently stuck in that niche. That is simply your starting place. Now that you have your niche, our next step is to build your brand. Your brand starts with a name.

Action Time:

1. Go to Chapter 7 of the free Film to Freedom accompanying course (you can access this course for free by going to www.videography-university.com/course) and print out the Videography Niche List.
2. Circle the five niches that you find most appealing.
3. Take your list of five circled niches and identify which niches you know a decision maker in.
    a. If you don't know a decision maker in one of the niches, pick the niche that you are most drawn to.
4. You now have the niche that you will be targeting for your videography business.

Section 4

Building Your Brand

Before starting this chapter, if you already have your videography business name and your brand assets (colors, logo, website, portfolio), then skip to Chapter 13, which talks about setting up the legal structure for your videography business. If you have already created the legal structure, then skip to Chapter 14, which talks about creating your portfolio. If you already have your portfolio for your niche, then skip this section and jump to Section 5: The 3-Phase Approach to 6-Figure Sales.

If you are just beginning on your journey and you don't have any of the above items, then proceed with this section. It is going to teach you how you can build your brand, set up the legal structure for your business, and create your portfolio. It all starts with creating your business name.

Chapter 11
CREATE A NAME

Naming your business is, in my opinion, one of the most over-analyzed aspects of starting a business. Don't let picking a name for your business delay you from building your business. Picking a name becomes a needless point of resistance to growing a business that can change your life. I'm guilty of letting this decision delay me from building my business. I remember taking weeks debating about what I should name my business. I thought small details in the name could be the difference between my company making hundreds of thousands of dollars in revenue or falling flat.

I remember putting a poll out on social media asking my friends if I should add an S or not onto the backend of the name I settled on. I then stalled another week debating on whether or not I should add the S. That was almost a month's worth of time that I could have been booking clients and earning money instead of wasting time. For those that are still skeptical, let's look at how two of the world's biggest companies came up with their names.

Steve Jobs and Steve Wozniak had the vision for the world's greatest computer company, but they didn't have a name.[5] What Jobs *did* have was a serious love for fruit. On a car ride home from the airport after a trip to an apple orchard in Oregon, Jobs threw out the idea to Wozniak, "What if we named our company 'Apple'?" He reportedly felt the name sounded fun, friendly, and unintimidating. Wozniak agreed, and the rest is history. A multibillion-dollar company named after a household fruit.

How about another one of the world's largest companies? Jeff Bezos had ambitions of creating the world's largest online bookstore, but what would he name it? In the early days of the internet, listings were ordered alphabetically. He wanted his company to be near the top of internet searches, so he decided the name would start with an A.[6] To the dictionary he went! He thumbed through the As in search of his company name. Eventually, he came across the word "Amazon." He thought to himself, "The Amazon River is the largest river in the world, and I want to create the largest online bookstore in the world." On November 1, 1994, Bezos registered the URL Amazon.com as a domain, and the rest is history.

Don't allow analysis paralysis over naming your business to postpone you from building your videography business. Below are three rules—the three-part test—I recommend you follow when deciding on your company name:

1. Make it easy to pronounce.
2. Make it easy to spell.
3. Make sure the domain is available.

1. *Make it easy to pronounce.*

You are going to have conversation after conversation about your business in the days, weeks, months, and years to come. You're going to be talking about it with friends, family, and clients. As you share about your business, your most powerful marketing engine will start running: word of mouth.

Word of mouth is the most powerful marketer out there. It's free, and it's highly effective. Imagine, your dearest friend Jennifer is sharing about the amazing work that you do with your dream client that she happens to have a relationship with. Jennifer has gone to bat for you and knocked the thing clear out of the park. This dream client is looking for video marketing services, and they are interested in reaching out to you to learn more about how you can meet their needs.

Jennifer goes in to seal the deal, and out comes, "Bob's company is [insert a mouthful of jumbled letters] ..." Jennifer sees the excitement in your dream client's eyes die alongside the possibility of the client trying to find your website next time they open a web browser on their phone. Save yourself from this scenario playing out, and give your company a name that is easy to pronounce. Think Apple, Amazon, Nike, Coke. Don't make it 15 syllables with a mixture of four languages.

2. *Make it easy to spell.*

Equally important to ease of pronunciation is ease of spelling. Let's run back that previous scenario. This time, let's say Jennifer is able to articulate the name of your company with ease, but let's say the spelling is misleading. For example, there was a trend for tech startups where they would make their name a common English word with a funky spelling. Think Atlys, Tumblr, Pixlr, and more. This trend was originally attributed to practical reasons as domain hoarders were taking domains for ransom in the early days of the internet, buying them up like pieces of real estate. After a while, this way of naming continued as more of a trend.

Unlike tech startups, when starting our videography businesses, most of us don't have millions of dollars to put into advertising our company and getting our name in front of clients. Let's say that you named your company, "Amzng Productions." When your friend brags about you to your dream client, the client is going to hear "Amazing Productions." When they google "Amazing Productions," they are either going to come up empty-handed, or worse yet, find your competition.

Save yourself from this possible scenario, and pick a name that is easy to spell and is spelled like it sounds.

3. *Make sure the domain is available.*

Lastly, make sure the domain is available. You've brainstormed a list of names, it's easy to spell, it's easy to pronounce, you would feel confident in standing on a stage in front of a thousand people and screaming it at the top of your lungs, now comes the critical step of making sure the domain name is available. The last thing you want to do is name your company just to find out that you can't even use the name as the domain for your website. Do not fear; there is an easy way to check to see if your desired domain is available.

Go to Chapter 11 of the free Film to Freedom companion course (you can access this course for free at www.videography-university.com/course) where we walk you through how to check and see if your desired domain name is available. After navigating to the link and checking your desired domain, if the domain is available, great! You've got your company name. At this point, you can go ahead and purchase the domain if you would like. You don't have to, but it might be a good idea to secure it now so that it does not get purchased by someone else later on. Domains are typically inexpensive. You can usually get a domain for around $12 per year or less.

If the site notifies you that your domain is taken, they might provide you with alternatives that start with something else or end with ".net," ".org," ".co," or some other ending instead of ".com." I recommend either making a slight adjustment to the part of the name before the "." or changing the name entirely. People view ".com" sites as the most trustworthy and you don't want to lose out on potential clients from someone being wary of a ".net" or ".org."

FILM TO FREEDOM

If the site notifies you that your domain is taken, you might also be provided the opportunity to use a broker service to try and bargain with the owner of the domain to sell it to you. I do not recommend going this route. It's possible that the owner of the domain will try to convince you to pay a large sum of money for it, and if you choose not to pay, you will still have to pay the broker fee anyway. Worst of all, this can delay you from taking the next step in your business. It's simply not worth the trouble or the cost. If the domain is taken, just move on to one of the other names you came up with.

Make it!

The worst thing that you can do is let naming your company be a barrier that prevents you from moving forward with building your business. Don't let this process take more than two days. Ultimately, if time goes by, and you hate your business's name, you can always rebrand in the future. What you can't do, or what would be very difficult to do, is land sales without having a business name.

The important thing is to name your company and keep moving forward. Follow the process I am about to outline, adhere to the three rules, then pick a name, and go with it. Before we jump into the naming workflow, I want to use my own situation to highlight how inconsequential the name of your company can be in the grand scheme of building a successful videography business.

My company is broken into two main brands: Ascension Productions and Optiko Productions. Ascension Productions was my original company name. This was when I started in wedding videography. I was happy with the name because it was easy to say and relatively easy to spell. Now comes the domain. When I started my wedding videography business, I knew so little about building websites that I unknowingly broke one of my own rules. I intended to purchase the domain, "www.ascension.productions.com," but instead I purchased the domain, "www.ascension.productions."

I added the period before "productions" because the name with no "." was already owned by somebody else. I assumed the domain provider added the ".com" automatically. Turns out, I had accidentally replaced the ".com" with ".productions." It was not until I did a Google search for "www.ascenion.productions.com" two weeks later that I discovered my mistake. I had already purchased the domain "www.ascension.productions," a Google Workspace for an email, and at the time, I was a poor kid fresh out of college, so there was no going back.

In spite of the domain debacle of 2019, to this day, I receive more wedding inquiries than I could take on. Moral of the story, not having the perfect name didn't prevent me from growing a business.

Additionally, my corporate videography business is "Optiko Productions." I got a little fancy with this one. It's derived from the word "optic," relating to "vision." I switched the C to a K because I liked the look of it better and added an

85

O on the end because I thought it sounded better. Sure, it's easy to pronounce, but I have to spell it out anytime someone is trying to find my business online. Has that stopped me from making six figures with my corporate videography business? No. Don't let over-analyzing your name slow you down in building your business.

Naming Your Business

It's time to name your business. In this section I'm going to outline two ways you can go about naming your videography business: the old school way, and the new school way.

The Old School Way

The Old School Way is a twist on the Jeff Bezos approach. Who knows; maybe you'll end up being the next Amazon. First step, grab a dictionary. If you don't have a dictionary, download the dictionary.com app on your phone. Since the internet is no longer ordered alphabetically, we don't need to worry about starting with the As. Let's make this a little bit personal; either pick the first letter of your first name or the first letter of your last name, and go to that letter in the dictionary.

Next, skim through the words that start with that letter in the dictionary, and write down any words that connect with you. It could be a personal connection, you like the way it sounds, or maybe it has some added meaning. Set a timer for 30 minutes and take no longer than 30 minutes. Shoot for a list of around 10 to 20 words. Fourth, look at that list, and add "productions" or "creative" after each word. Adding "productions" or "creative" will indicate to clients the type of business you are. See which words sound the best as a name. If one of the words sparks another word or set of words, write them down. From here, narrow down your list to around five names. Once you have your top five, put them through the three-part test that we reviewed earlier.

1. Is it easy to pronounce?
2. Is it easy to spell?
3. Is the domain available?

If the first name passes the test, congratulations, you have the name of your videography business. If the first name doesn't meet all three of the requirements, move on to the next name. Keep repeating the process until you have a winner. Just remember, make it! Don't take more than two days picking your business name. If the old school approach doesn't jive with you, go with the new school approach.

New School Approach

Navigate to Chapter 11 of the free Film to Freedom companion course (you can access this course by going to www.videography-university.com/course). In this section of the course, you will find a great free website that will provide you with a unique list of names and even provide you with ideas on logo designs. Once you are redirected to the website, simply follow the directions provided to generate a list of unique names. Scroll through the list, and write down any that stick out to you.

Once you have a list of around 10 names, run them through the three-part test provided earlier. Once you have a name that passes all three parts of the test, you've got your business name.

Once you have your name, go ahead and purchase the domain if you would like. Once again, this should only cost around $12 per year. Once you have the domain locked down, give yourself a big pat on the back because you have officially named your business and you're one step closer to realizing your dream of building a six-figure videography business. The next step is to build out your brand assets.

Action Time:

Follow the old school or new school approach to naming your videography business. Go to Chapter 11 of the free Film to Freedom comapnion course (you can access this course for free at www.videography-university.com/course). All of the resources needed to create your business name will be there along with an accompanying video walking you through using each resource.

1. Don't take more than two days naming your videography business!

Chapter 12

BRAND ASSETS

You have your company name, now it's time to build out your brand. At this stage, there are five main assets that you will want to create for your brand:

1. Brand colors
2. Logo
3. Headshot
4. Website
5. Portfolio

Brand Colors

Brand colors are key to professional design for your branded content. Whether this be business cards or your website, having brand colors keeps things consistent and earns you credibility in the eyes of your target audience. This is another opportunity for resistance. Don't let this delay you from building your video production business.

To find color pallets that you can use for your business go to Chapter 12 of the free Film to Freedom companion course (you can access the companion course for free at www.videography-university.com/course). In this section of the course you will find resources that will help you select your brand colors. At the end of the day, don't overcomplicate it. Once again, you can always go back and rebrand later if you want to change colors.

Logo

Next, it's time to create your logo. A logo is an asset that you are going to use over and over again. Your logo is going to be plastered alongside your company name and will be one of the first things your clients think of when they think of your company. When creating your logo, focus on two things:

1. Make it simple.
2. Make it applicable.

Simplicity is key when creating your logo. The best logos are not overly complicated. Do me a favor and close your eyes. If you actually just closed your eyes and then realized you couldn't read the next sentence with your eyes closed, please DM me, "You got me!" on Instagram. If you didn't close your eyes, please DM me, "Nice try, buddy!" I want honesty here, people! This will be a fun experiment. But seriously, I'm going to provide a series of company names, and I want you to think of their logo. See how many you can get:

1. Nike
2. McDonalds
3. Apple
4. Starbucks
5. Pepsi
6. Google
7. Twitter
8. YouTube

How many were you able to get? Most people can quickly picture these logos in their minds. What do all of these logos have in common? They're simple. They don't have dozens of colors and intricate designs. Most of these logos are one or two colors and could easily be drawn by a kindergartner. A key to an effective logo is making it simple.

Additionally, a great logo is applicable to your industry. It's helpful to have a logo that people will see and immediately think, "Video." This way, when somebody who is in need of videography services sees your logo, it will immediately catch their eye. You don't want to miss out on prospects because someone saw your logo and thought your business didn't have anything to do with videography.

If you want to create your own logo, you can use a resource such as Canva, Adobe Photoshop, or Adobe Illustrator to do so. If this is the case, I recommend first using a resource to get some ideas flowing. Go to Chapter 12 of the free Film to Freedom companion course (you can access the companion course for free at www.videography-university.com/course) and follow the prompts to generate logos. Use those designs to get further ideas. When creating your own logo, just follow the two rules I previously mentioned:

1. Make it simple.
2. Make it applicable.

If logo creation is not something that you are proficient in, what I recommend most people do is to pay a small amount of money for professional logo design. This doesn't have to be an expensive process. You can pay $5 dollars and get a great logo. In the free Film to Freedom companion course, we have outlined steps to that you can use to have someone create a logo for you. Go to Chapter 12 of the companion course to access these resources.

This route is going to save you a lot of time and ultimately provide you with a great logo for a fraction of the hassle compared to creating your own. I created both of my own logos for my businesses and have since paid someone to create new ones that I felt were more professional.

Headshot

Now that you have your logo, it's time to capture a professional headshot. People do business with people they know, like, and trust. One of the best ways to start to build a relationship with clients is by helping them put a face to your name. A professional headshot is key to branding in this technological world. Tests have shown that adding a headshot into your email signature can increase your response rate by up to 20%.[7] Put yourself in the best spot possible by capturing a professional headshot to use in your branding.

If you have the skills to capture the headshot yourself, do so. If you have a friend that has the skills to do it for you, leverage that relationship. Focus on capturing a sharp, professional headshot, where you're showcasing a welcoming smile. Dress nice, find a clean background, and show off that smile. For more resources on capturing a professional headshot, go to Chapter 12 of the Film to Freeom companion course. A professional headshot can show your clients that you're welcoming and friendly. Next, it's time to build your website.

Website

Building a website can be a significant point of resistance. Remember, our goal is to remove as much resistance as possible so that you keep moving forward with building your business. Your website doesn't need to be the Mona Lisa of websites. There are three keys that I want you to focus on with your website:

1. Create a homepage where you tell your website visitors:
    • Who you are
    • The industry you serve

- How you can help them
2. Create a "Work" or "Portfolio" page (more on this in Chapter 14 of this section)
3. Create a "Contact Us" page

That's it. That's all you need to start off with your website.

Once again, you don't need to spend exorbitant sums of money purchasing a domain, hosting your website, and paying someone to design it. There are many inexpensive options for building and hosting a website. Most of them are around $10 to $15 per month. Some of these include Squarespace, Wix, Webflow, and Weebly. To get started creating your website, go to Chapter 12 of the free Film to Freedom companion course. In this section we provide a free video detailing the breakdown of an effective website for your videography business. Structure your website in the same way, and you will have an effective website to send clients to.

You've got your company name, and you've got your brand assets, so now it's time to take care of some logistics: How do you want to structure your business?

Action Time:

1. Create your brand colors. Go to Chapter 12 of the free companion course to get help creating yours. You can access the companion course for free at www.videography-university.com/course.
2. Create a logo. Go to Chapter 12 of the free companion course to create your logo.

3. Capture a headshot. Go to Chapter 12 of the free companion course for resources to help you capture a professional headshot.

4. Create your website. Go to Chapter 12 of the free companion course to find resources to help you create your website.

Chapter 13

STRUCTURE YOUR BUSINESS

First, I want to start by adding a disclaimer that I am not a lawyer, and you should not take my words as legal advice. I recommend consulting with a lawyer prior to making any legal decisions in regards to your business. Additionally, in this section we will be discussing legal structures for businesses. This is going to be unique to where you live. Most of the items discussed are applicable to those living in the United States. If you live outside of the United States, you might have different legal structures for businesses. Once again, I recommend consulting with a lawyer for advice based on your location. With all of that being said, I want to provide you with a pivotal moment in my business journey, when I decided to create an LLC for my business.

I used to think that running a business was as easy as creating a name and getting the word out there. Sitting where I am today, I now understand why they say the first two things you should do when you start a business is get an accountant and get a lawyer.

My first year doing videography on the side was a mess when it came to separating my business from my personal life. My personal calendar was also my business calendar, my personal email was also my business email, and my personal bank account was also my business bank account. When I hit tax season, I discovered that I had created a nightmare.

I stayed up late every night for a week sifting through my checking account, looking at every purchase I had made, then surveying the bank codes to try to figure out if that had been a business expense or a personal expense. I worked tirelessly to track down any and all receipts that I could find as I didn't know I needed to save all of my receipts from throughout the year. On top of this, I spent days retracing my driving record from the year to identify what miles were to be counted as "business miles" and what miles were "personal." These are things they don't teach you in school.

It was a nightmare compiling all of the information necessary to pay my taxes for the year. What a sad state of affairs. I made it through the tax debacle, and not long after, I had a conversation with a fellow videographer who was operating a videography business of his own. We were talking shop, and he mentioned to me how he had designated his business as an LLC so that he could separate his business expenses from his personal expenses and prevent a disgruntled client from suing him for his personal assets.

Shivers went down my spine. This harrowing story had me doing some serious self-reflection for my business the next day. That week, I took steps to set up my business as an LLC. A month later, I turned my business into an LLC, created a checking account for myself through my bank, and started using QuickBooks Self Employed, a bookkeeping platform that allows you to keep track of your taxes one hundred times more easily than doing it all on your own.

Moral of the story: Once you have your business name, consider setting up a legal structure for your business. There are three main business types for small businesses:

1. Sole Proprietorship
2. Limited Liability Company (LLC)
3. Corporation

Let's break these down a bit further.

Sole Proprietorship: Sole proprietorships are the most common type of small businesses and also provide the least amount of distinction between the business and your personal assets. Really the only cost with designating your business as a sole proprietorship is if you decided to register your business name with your state. Outside of that, *you* are the business. For this reason, you also carry all of the liability of the business. If someone were to sue your business for any reason, they would be suing you directly. This type of business is the easiest to set up but also provides you the least amount of protection.

Limited Liability Company (LLC): An LLC takes a little bit more work to set up than a sole proprietorship, but it also provides you with more protection. Structuring your business as an LLC allows you to protect your personal assets if someone were to make a claim against your business. This means people can't come after your personal assets if they were to sue you for some sort of grievance. There is a filing fee associated with creating an LLC, which generally runs from around $100 to $800 depending on what state your business is in. (Sorry, California.)

Another added benefit of the LLC distinction is that it remains very easy to file your taxes if you are a single member LLC, i.e., you are the sole owner. The process is very similar to filing taxes for yourself as if you were just reporting your own individual income. This is the business structure that I decided to create for my business when I became serious about building my videography business.

Corporations (C-Corp and S-Corp): Corporations are the most complex of the three business structures outlined in this chapter. A corporation is considered a legal entity that is completely separate and distinct from the people who own or run the business. Typically, larger businesses elect to utilize this business structure as it can be easier to manage payroll with multiple employees than an LLC. Filing taxes is more complex with a corporation as the corporation is its own taxpaying entity. In addition, there are more costs and steps to setting up a corporation than the other two business structures.

With all of this being said, I found an LLC to be the sweet spot of protection, simplicity, and cost effectiveness when I set up the legal structure for my business. Do your own research, consider meeting with a lawyer, and figure out what structure would work best for you and your business. Just understand that there are implications with whichever structure you choose, so be sure to make the right decision for you.

The other thing I would highly consider doing is setting up a business account to separate your personal and business transactions. This is going to make your life easier come tax season. In addition, with most major banks, there is no fee to set up a business account. Usually if you maintain a small balance within the account, utilize a direct deposit into the account, or maintain a certain number of transactions each month, you will not receive monthly fees for having the account. I recommend calling your bank to see what kind of accounts they offer for small businesses.

If you are looking for a bank that provides great options for small businesses, I highly recommend Chase Bank. They are a national bank and have many different tools to help small businesses succeed. Chase is who I set up my business account with when I created my LLC.

My last note when it comes to bookkeeping is don't forget about taxes. Sometimes I see newly created small business owners forget that they have to pay taxes on the money that they earn. Don't fall into the trap of spending what you earn. Put money aside for taxes. Before I ever transferred money into my personal account, I set aside 30% into a secondary business account. I used this account as my tax account. Before anything came into my personal account, 30% would go into my tax account so that I knew, at the end of each quarter, I had money set aside for my taxes.

Generally, 30% gave me money left over. I considered this leftover money as my self-employed tax return at the end of each year. You might be thinking, "Why do you keep saying "each quarter, Grant? Taxes aren't due until the end of the year." Another nuance of being a business owner is that you are responsible for paying quarterly taxes (another thing they don't teach you in school). This is very important to know when running your own business. When people work for a company, typically they are unaware of this tax payment, but as a business owner you are responsible for paying these taxes for your business. These taxes consist of your income tax and your self-employment tax.

Your income tax is dependent upon income that you earn that quarter. Your self-employment tax is more cut and dry and, depending on the year, is typically around 15.3%. As you can imagine, with all tax-related and legal items, there are nuances to these percentages based on where you live, how much you make, etc. The important thing to know is that they exist and that you figure out how they are going to apply to you. For this reason, I highly recommend doing research on your own, talking to an accountant, or better yet, do both.

Lastly, one tool that has been a lifesaver for me when it comes to invoicing, accounting, tracking mileage, and keeping tabs on my monthly income is QuickBooks Self-Employed. This piece of software changed my life when I stumbled upon it a year into my business. It is low cost at $15/month and allows you to send electronic invoices with extremely low processing rates, track mileage automatically using the app, and keep tabs on all of your income and expenses. QuickBooks Self-Employed is a tool that changed my business when I started using it. I highly recommend looking into this tool for your business.

You have your company name, you have your brand assets, and you've set up the legal structure for your business, so now it's time to show prospective clients what you can do for them. It's time to create your portfolio. This is a real chicken-or-the-egg type situation—how can you show clients your portfolio if you haven't had any clients to give you work to create a portfolio? Fear not, this next chapter will outline the exact steps to take to create a portfolio, build your client base, and start earning your way toward a six-figure videography business.

Action Time:

1. Review options for business structures and identify which option is best for you. Consider meeting with a lawyer for advice.
2. Understand tax implications for running your own business, and create a tax plan that works for you. Consider meeting with an accountant for advice. Make sure you save appropriately for taxes!

Chapter 14
BUILD YOUR PORTFOLIO

Two Cents Over Minimum Wage

I used to think people would hire you for the work that you *could do*. Now I know that people hire you for the work that you *have done*.

I was a freshman in high school, and it was time for me to get my first job. I had ambitions of purchasing my first camera, and I knew that I was going to have to save up a nice chunk of change to make those dreams a reality. Fortunately for me, I knew exactly where I wanted to work. A few weeks prior, I'd walked into one of my favorite places in the world, the movie theater, and there, next to the ticketing booth, was a sign, "Now Hiring: Theatre Usher." That was it; that was the job.

I took home a flier to learn more about the position. It was a dream come true. You passed out tickets to moviegoers at the front of the theater. What could be better than welcoming moviegoers as they stepped into the magical world that is the movie theater? On top of that, as a theater usher, you had the benefit of unlimited tickets to movies, half off concessions, and on slow days when you weren't working, I heard they even let you screen old movies they had in the back. This was the job for me.

The application was short: a letter outlining prior experience indicating why you would be a good fit for the job. But I had no prior work experience. "No problem," I thought to myself, "I will simply write a letter telling them how passionate I am about the role, and they'll see why I'm the perfect fit!"

I drafted up a beauty of a letter telling them my dreams and ambitions of one day working in movies and how passionate I was about the theater-going experience. With my letter in hand, my mom dropped me off at the theater. I walked in and said that I would like to apply for the open theater usher position. The manager came out, greeted me with a big smile, and asked for my letter of prior experience. I proudly handed off my letter and shook his hand, confident that the next time we shook hands, it would be him congratulating me on getting the role. I walked out of the theater, head held high. The next day, I sat by our home phone anxiously awaiting a call from the manager.

Crickets.

A few more days went by ... no call.

I asked my mom to take me back to the theater so that I could ask the manager if there was any update on the role. I arrived at the theater, opened the door, and to my horror, the "Now Hiring" sign was gone. I looked up, and there standing behind the ticketing booth was a boy I had never seen before. He was wearing a stark black uniform that held no sign of wrinkles or stains.

I walked around the corner to see the manager. He greeted me with that same big smile. I asked him if he had any update on the position I'd applied for. He said, "I'm sorry, buddy, we just filled the role a few days ago." I was devastated. He read my face like a book. "I'm sorry, bud!" he said. "Your letter was great! Unfortunately, the person we hired just had a bit more experience than you."

I spent the rest of that summer busting my butt in the kitchen of a local restaurant making two cents an hour over minimum wage. No tips.

I learned a valuable lesson that day. People don't hire you for the work that you *can do*, they hire you for the work that you *have done*.

Building Your Portfolio

In videography, your "résumé" is your portfolio. When a client is interested in hiring you, they'll want to see previous work showcasing the kind of work you can do for them. Business owners want to know that their investment will provide a return, and marketers want to know that your videos are going to drive results.

Let's say a business owner is interested in a video for the homepage of their website. They want a video that shows who they are, what they do, and how they can help their clients. They're planning to spend a few thousand dollars on the video. Now let's look at two hypothetical situations: We have Joe Nuthintashow, a videographer without a portfolio, and we have Peter Portfullio, a videographer with a beautiful portfolio.

The business owner reaches out to Joe. Joe says, "We can produce that video for you for $5,000." The business owner asks to see examples of Joe's previous work, but he has none. Joe promises that he has all the skills and tools necessary to get the job done.

The business owner reaches out to Peter who has a beautiful portfolio showcasing well composed shots and crisp audio. Peter shows him the portfolio piece and tells him how the client integrated the video into their website. Peter pitches $7,000 for the project. The business owner asks where they can sign.

What's the difference? Joe Nuthintashow told the business owner the work he *could* do for him. Peter Portfullio showed the business owner the work he *had* done for a previous client. Peter had a proven track record instilling confidence in the business owner. The business owner knew their investment was going to get them a quality product that would earn them future business.

You've built the mentality, you know your niche, you have your brand assets. Now it's time to create your portfolio.

The first step to creating your portfolio is figuring out what kind of videos will be in your portfolio. What kind of videos should be in your portfolio? Well, what's your niche? When I branched into corporate videos for small- to medium-sized businesses, I needed a brand-new portfolio. At that time, the only niche I was in was wedding videography, so the only portfolio I had was of wedding videos. I knew that I couldn't show a wedding video to a business owner and expect them to hire me to create a corporate video for their business. I needed to create an example corporate video as a portfolio piece to show to business owners.

Maybe your niche is creating social media videos for CrossFit gyms. In that case, your portfolio should consist of short, highly engaging videos of CrossFit gyms that are optimized for social media consumption.

Maybe your niche is product videos for medical equipment manufacturers. In that case, your portfolio should consist of videos that highlight features and uses of medical equipment.

Maybe your niche is conference highlight videos for corporate conferences. In that case, your portfolio should consist of videos that highlight corporate conferences.

Whatever the case may be, I want you to grab a sheet of paper and write down the three questions below and put in your answers, or you can go to Chapter 13 of the free companion course and print off the PDF we've created for you (you can access the free companion course at www.videography-university.com/course).

Write:

1. The title for the type of video. This is what you would call it when referencing it with clients, e.g., Corporate Website Video, Social Media Video, Product Demo Video, etc.

2. Who your target client is, e.g., real estate agent, dental practice owner, marketing director of manufacturing company, etc.

3. What the video would consist of, e.g., interviews, B-roll, voiceover, animation, etc.

Now, it might feel like you're caught in a chicken-or-egg situation. How do you create a portfolio for someone when nobody will hire you because you don't have a portfolio? Next, I'm going to show you how to create your portfolio while securing new potential clients at the same time.

From Free Video to $100,000

Rewind to when I was a year into my second job out of college. I was working every day at a job that checked all of the boxes for most, but every second I was working this job, all I wanted to do was work on building my videography business. I knew that videography was my passion, and I knew that I wanted videography to be my full-time career, but I had one big problem: I had no idea how to find clients.

I knew that I wanted to shoot corporate videos, but what business owner in their right mind would pay someone thousands of dollars to create a video for them when they had no proven track record? I knew I could do the job if someone would give me the chance. That's when it hit me: Maybe someone won't pay me thousands of dollars to create a video for them when I didn't have a portfolio, but I bet I could find someone who wanted the type of video I wanted to produce, and I bet if I offered to do it for free, they would say yes. And I bet once I had that portfolio piece to show other business owners, they would pay me for the same type of video.

That night I jumped onto Google and typed in "dental practices near me." A list of dental practices populated my screen. I worked my way through the list, clicking on each practice's website, checking to see if they had an "About Us" video on their homepage. If they didn't, I checked to see if I could find the email for the practice owner or administrative assistant. After working my way through a few websites, I had a list of emails from three practices who didn't have a video on their homepage. I sent the first one the following email:

I woke up the next morning, started work at my 9-to-5, and on my lunch break checked my inbox. I had the following email:

I couldn't believe it. Maybe this wasn't a paid project, but reaching out to a business and hearing that they were interested in my services was a shot of adrenaline. I was one step closer to creating my portfolio. I emailed the practice manager back, we set up a time to hop on a call, and after our call, we had a date scheduled to shoot the video.

Shoot day came, and I was overwhelmingly excited. I closed my laptop after work, loaded my SUV with my equipment, and rushed to the practice. I opened the front door and was welcomed by a warm greeting from the practice manager. I set up all of the equipment for the shoot, interviewed the practice manager, front desk manager, and lead dentist.

After the interviews, I captured B-roll of the practice. Once I wrapped up the B-roll, I packed up, thanked the practice manager, and headed home. After a few days of editing, I sent the finished video to the practice manager. They were thrilled with the video. After a few adjustments,

I sent them the finished video, and they responded with the following email:

I had my first portfolio piece, and now I had four testimonials that I could use to market to future businesses.

The excitement from producing my portfolio piece faded when I had the sobering realization that now I needed to convince a business to actually *pay* me for a video. The next day I went back to my list of emails for dental practices. I copied and pasted the second email on the list and sent them the following email (that was about two times too wordy):

The next day on my lunch break, I opened my laptop, all the while telling myself not to get my hopes too high. To my disbelief, the following email was sitting in my inbox:

I couldn't believe it. A business owner had seen my work and was interested in hiring me to create a video for his dental practice. I called the owner, we talked through his vision for the video, finalized the details, set up a date to shoot, and created the video. He and his team were excited about the first draft. After a few revisions, we had the finished product and the lead dentist was thrilled to put his new video to work.

To this day, that video sits proudly on the homepage of his website, working for his practice day and night, giving prospective patients an inside look into the care that they provide for their patients. With that single video, I made three weeks' worth of my salary at my 9-to-5. That is 120 hours' worth of work at my full-time job for 20 total hours shooting and editing that video.

I showed that video to the marketing director for a tech organization looking for coverage of a conference they were hosting in New York. That turned into a $5,000 project. The marketing director for a healthcare IT company saw the video on LinkedIn and hired me for a $3,000 project. I showed the video from the conference in New York to an organization looking for testimonials for a conference they were hosting in Columbus, Ohio, and that turned into a $4,000 project. I showed those testimonials to another business owner looking for coverage of a conference he was putting on in Columbus. That turned into another $4,000 project. I showed the dental practice video to a marketing director of another company. That turned into a $10,000 project (my first five-figure project), and that project then turned into more projects for that company that combined for another $12,000 over the next year. More and more projects came in until, in roughly a year's time, that free video I shot for a dental practice turned into $70,000 worth of projects.

At that same time, I saw an opportunity for me to serve clients with a different type of video content. I was creating one-time videos for clients for their marketing channels, but I saw so many businesses who could benefit from continued video content for their social media pages. This was different from content I had produced before, but I knew that there was a need for it. The first thing I needed to do was create an example of this type of content in my portfolio to show to prospective clients.

My dear friend, Ryan Willis, was just getting his footing as a real estate agent at the time and was looking for ways to grow his client base. I knew he could benefit from the type of videos I was looking to make, so I asked him if he would be willing to let me create a series of videos for his social media pages. I would give him the finished videos to use for marketing, and all I asked for in return was a testimonial and his permission to use the videos on my website to market to future clients.

He was in.

The next week we captured the video content. I spent a few days editing the footage. The finished product was exactly what I was hoping for, and he was thrilled to have the new videos to market his business.

A few weeks went by, and I got a text from Ryan. "Hey, another real estate agent I work with saw the videos on my social media pages, and they wanted your number to talk about videos for their social media." That day I received a call from the agent, we talked about their vision, my process, and in a few days, I locked in my first monthly retainer for continued video content for $1,000 per month. After a few months this retainer turned into a $1,500-per-month retainer. After six months, that client had another colleague who wanted the same content for their social media. Another $1,000 per month. I was now making $2,500 per month in monthly retainer work on top of everything I was making from my other projects. The free video I created for Ryan turned into $2,500 in consistent monthly income.

That year, those two free videos alone earned me just under $100,000. The relationships I built from those videos continue to bring me more and more work. This is the power of a method called free-to-fee.

Now, you've probably heard people in the industry say, "You should never work for free!" I agree that you should not allow yourself to be taken advantage of, and trust me, there are plenty of people out there that would happily take advantage of you and your skills. That is why it is important that you abide by three principles when utilizing the free-to-fee method to create your portfolio.

1. **You** call the shots.
2. **You** are provided a testimonial.
3. **You** are free to use the video for marketing purposes wherever **you** would like.

You Call the Shots.

When people say you should never work for free, I agree with them that you should not (I don't like saying never) work for free if you're not the one calling the shots. The people who ask *you* to work for free for *them* are usually looking to get whatever they can out of you and provide you with little to nothing in return. Avoid these people like the plague. They'll waste your time and leave you frustrated. If someone asks you to do work for free, there better be some massive alternate form of compensation in store for you. I've been on both sides of this equation, and I have learned my lesson the hard way.

A real estate agent once asked me to shoot a video for their brokerage, although she said they didn't have any money for the video. Working for free for this agent was a bad move on my part; I later found out she was making over $500,000 in commissions per year. She said she would market me to her other business partners in return, and I was wary but thought, "Maybe those relationships will turn into some well-paying jobs in the future." I took on the project. I shot the project, edited the video, sent it over to the agent. The agent asked for revision after revision after revision. I was fed up with the project by the fifth round of revisions. Finally, the agent was satisfied with the product. I spent a total of around 40 hours on the video and never saw a dime from any of her colleagues. I doubt she ever even mentioned me to them.

That's an example of a project and client that is asking for free work that you do not want to take on. Now let's look at the flip side of the coin.

After my first year of being full-time, I decided it was a wise idea to join my local Chamber of Commerce to network with other local business owners. I submitted my application, spoke with the onboarding team, and was accepted into the local chamber. The day after I became a member, I received a call from a marketing representative for the chamber. She asked me if I would be interested in shooting a video for the chamber in exchange for my chamber fees being waived. I told her that while I appreciated the offer, the chamber fees were only $300, and I charged around $3,000 for the type of video she was looking for.

She said she would put together a list of promotions for my business that the chamber would cover to make the exchange of services more even. I told her to send the adjusted offer over to me. The next day, she sent me an email outlining the coverage of my chamber fees as well as 15-plus promotions the chamber would be covering for my business in exchange for the video. Those promotions have turned into multiple projects that have paid out well over the $3,000 I would have charged for the video. The chamber representative was also a joy to work with.

Moral of the story: If you're shooting a video for free but you're not the one in the driver's seat, make sure that the project is going to be worth your time.

Ultimately, when it comes to free work, you should be the one calling the shots. When I offered to shoot the video for free for the first dental practice, that was because I knew what type of videos I wanted to offer to future clients, and I needed a portfolio piece to show them. I was in the driver's seat. I reached out to them and offered my services in exchange for the type of video that I wanted to shoot. The practice owner agreed. They were provided with a great video to help book more patients, and I was provided with a portfolio piece that I could use to market to future clients along with a testimonial from a well-respected individual in the market I was looking to break into. This was a win-win situation. I knew it would be a win-win because I was calling the shots.

You Are Provided a Testimonial.

Testimonials are one of the most powerful tools for gaining credibility as a business. When prospective clients see words from one of your past clients about how great you were to work with and how awesome of a video you made, you're going to build trust with them. According to a study from Wyzowl, "95% of people say that reviews—whether positive, or negative—influence their purchasing decisions."[8] If you have a glowing testimonial from a respected past client on your website, this is going to do wonders for you in booking future projects. When you offer a free video, set the expectation that, if the client is happy with the finished product, they will provide you with a testimonial.

I mentioned earlier that the free video I created for Ryan turned into two monthly retainer contracts. Prior to working together, the second of the two clients reached out to me via email inquiring about social media videos. We jumped on a phone call, and I asked her about the videos she wanted for her social media channels. She said, "Really, I was hoping to have the same type of videos you've been creating for Jeff." Jeff was her colleague who recommended me to her. "That's easy," I thought to myself. I told her I would put together a few packages for her, we set up a time to review the packages, and we ended the call.

I recreated the packages I made for her colleague with a few tweaks to better match her brand. A few days later, we met to review the options. As we were talking, it seemed as though she wasn't fully present. It felt as though she was waiting for the meeting to be over.

After I ran her through the packages, I asked her if she had any questions. She said, "Nope! Jeff has loved the work you've done for him. If Jeff's excited about what you've done for him, I trust you. Which package did Jeff go with?"

I was overselling the entire time. The client was sold from the moment her colleague told her how excited he was about the work I created for him. His testimonial did more than any sales pitch I could ever create. At that point, it was just up to me not to screw it up. This is the power of testimonials. Be sure to require a testimonial from clients that you do free work for.

You are free to use the video for marketing purposes wherever you would like.

The main objective of shooting your first video for free is to get a portfolio piece. This means that you need to be able to share the finished video wherever and whenever you would like. You need to be able to post it to your website for website visitors to see, you need to be able to post it to social media for your social media followers to see, and you need to be able to share it with prospective clients when performing outreach for new projects.

121

I highly recommend that you set this understanding for all of your projects as growing your body of work is going to be a big driver behind you growing your business. Set this expectation with the client in the initial outreach.

Additionally, this provides reasonable justification to the prospective client. If you were to reach out to someone offering a free video without any justification, they would likely be skeptical, asking themselves what your angle is. By being upfront and saying, "I would like to shoot a video for free for your business, and in exchange, I would like to be able to use the video for marketing purposes and a testimonial if you are pleased with the finished product," the client is going to understand that it is a mutually beneficial relationship and you have no hidden agenda. This further builds trust.

Once you have laid out these three ground rules, it's time to reach out to your target client. You already have your niche, now it's about getting into contact with decision makers. Don't overcomplicate this step. Determine where your target audience is, show up, and provide them with an irresistible offer. I have reached out to businesses successfully via email, LinkedIn, Instagram, and the ever-terrifying in-person. For email and social media outreach templates, go to Chapter 14 of the free Film to Freedom companion course to access outreach templates you can use when reaching out to prospective clients (you can access the companion course for free at www.videography-university.com/course).

Use those templates to get started, and adjust them accordingly to fit your niche, your goals, and your personality. Don't be discouraged if you don't hear back the first few times you reach out. I was lucky enough to receive a response from the first two businesses I reached out to. Those conversion rates are not normal. Shoot for a ten-to-one outreach-to-response ratio. If you keep reaching out, I promise you will hear back, and you will lock in your first portfolio piece. Once you have your first portfolio piece, you're ready to start driving sales. In this next chapter, we'll talk about the three-phase process to six-figure sales.

Action Time:

1. Create your portfolio outline. Go to Chapter 14 of the Film to Freedom companion course and fill out the portfoli document (you can access the companion course for free at www.videography-university.com/course).

2. Reach out to your target client, and offer a free video in exchange for a testimonial and the ability to use the video for all marketing purposes. Go to Chapter 14 of the companion course for templates you can use to reach out to your target client.

3. Continue outreach until you land a client to create your first portfolio piece.

Section 5:

The 3-Phase Approach to 6-Figure Sales

Chapter 15

THE IMPORTANCE OF SALES

I want you to think back on your "why." What did your "why" consist of? What are the reasons you're motivated to build a six-figure videography business? Was it to achieve financial success for yourself? Was it to achieve financial security for your family or future family? Was it to unlock a life of freedom? Personal freedom to be your own boss. To go on vacations when you want? Financial freedom to afford nice things? A new car? A nice house? Freedom to buy yourself more leisure time?

Whatever your "why" is, envision you've already fulfilled it. Picture your life as you've realized all of those "why's". You're driving that car you wanted to purchase. You're relaxing on the beach, toes in the sand, cold beverage in your hand, on that vacation you wanted to be able to have the work flexibility to take. You're listening to the sweet sounds of your children's laughter as they chase your dog around the house that you were able to afford and had the time to enjoy with them.

Do you feel the stress melt away as you picture yourself in this moment? Do you feel the inner warmth it brings, feeling the personal satisfaction of achieving your goals? Do you experience the inner peace of being content with the life you've built?

There is one thing that you need in order to achieve your "why": sales.

Sales is the most important part of every business. Sales is the bottom line, the thing that keeps businesses afloat, the item that makes personal dreams a reality for those that benefit from them. Without sales, you have no business. With sales, the world is at your fingertips.

Often, throughout society, sales gets a bad rap. When people think of sales, visions of slicked-back hair and a painted-on smile come to mind. Often, we imagine the old cliché of a used car salesman. Someone chomping at the bit to get your signature, collect a commission, and cash your check before your patched-up clunker exits the lot and falls to pieces. It's critical that we reframe this mindset. I'm here to provide you with a new definition for sales.

Sales Defined

When you think of sales, I want you to think of one word: partnership. A videographer who views sales as a one-way transaction is going to have a short-lived career that is going to end in an impressive show of negative word of mouth. The truth of the matter is, sales is a partnership. In its full definition, I want you to think of sales as an exchange of goods or services that results in a mutually beneficial outcome.

As videographers, we are offering our time, talent, skills, and gear to produce an agreed-upon video for a client in exchange for financial compensation. The goal is to provide the client with the end product we've agreed upon in exchange for money. This is a partnership. The moment we stop thinking of sales as mutually beneficial is the moment we see our business decline. There are two distinct reasons for this:

1. The least expensive client to get is the client you have.
2. Word of mouth is the best route to driving new sales.

Securing new business takes time and money. Finding qualified clients and landing those clients is a process. It takes marketing dollars and time prospecting. The cheapest way to get more clients is repeat business. According to the Harvard Business Review, it can be five to 25 times more expensive to earn a new client than it is to retain an existing one.[9] Happy customers buy again. This means you're not starting from scratch every time you finish a project.

In addition, the most effective route to getting new business is word-of-mouth referrals from previous satisfied clients. People do business with people they trust. A trusted referral from a past client is better than any marketing dollars you can spend. According to a study by Nielsen, 92% of consumers around the world say that they trust recommendations from people they know over any other form of advertising.[10] If you want to grow your business, create happy customers.

Does creating happy clients make you feel like a slimy salesperson? I hope not! Make this partnership your focus, and sales should never be a fear of yours. Once you begin to feel the sliminess of bad sales, focus back on this question: "Am I building a partnership with my clients and working to build a mutually beneficial relationship?" If the answer is yes, don't allow society's ill-conceived notions of sales to creep into your head. If the answer is no, identify what needs to change in order for the partnership to be mutually beneficial.

Now that we've defined sales and discussed how important it is, let's talk about the three-phase approach to six-figure sales. This approach consists of (1) outbound sales, (2) inbound sales, and (3) repeat sales. Think of these phases as the legs of a stool. They each play an important part in keeping the stool upright. Without one, the stool would fall over. This is the same with your business. It is important that each of these areas is given adequate time and attention. By following the steps outlined in the next three chapters, you will be able to build a six-figure videography business. It all starts with outbound sales.

Chapter 16
OUTBOUND SALES

Outbound sales are sales that you are securing through active outreach. Many videographers try to build their business solely on inbound sales. They wait for prospects to come to them, and when not enough people come knocking on their door, they give up on their business and blame it on bad luck.

The simple fact is that outbound sales should be the life-blood of your business. You should constantly be seeking out new business through outbound sales. You don't have full control over the number of clients that seek out your business through inbound leads, but you have full control over the efforts you put into outbound sales.

This is what separates the average videographer from those that make an impressive living with their business. The good news is that I don't see a significant number of videographers that have the knowledge or drive to perform effective outbound sales, so this is an easy opportunity to set yourself above the rest. In this chapter, I hope to provide you with a structure that allows you to scale your videography business to unimaginable heights.

The outbound sales process can be broken down into three stages:

1. Identifying Qualified Leads
2. Outreach
3. Providing Solutions

Identifying Qualified Leads

The first step in the process is to identify qualified leads. You could execute perfectly on your outreach, your presentation, and your closing, but if the lead is not in a position to purchase, all of the effort will be wasted. Save yourself time, energy, and heartache upfront by qualifying leads.

A qualified lead is a client that could benefit from your services and is in a position to buy. How do you identify who a qualified lead is for your niche? First, take a look at your niche and ask yourself, "Who are the decision makers in my niche?" Decision makers are the people who make the purchasing decisions. These are the people who have the power to say, "Let's go ahead and move forward with this video project. Send me the invoice for the deposit."

Let's look at a few different industries to talk about what this looks like practically speaking. Let's say your niche is producing corporate videos for chiropractic offices. In this case, your decision makers would be owners of chiropractic offices. Let's look at another example. Say your niche is creating social media videos for real estate agents. In this case, your decision makers would be real estate agents. Now, not all decision makers for your niche will be qualified leads. What are additional characteristics that make someone a qualified lead? If a decision maker is not in a position to purchase, then they are not a qualified lead. Let's look at our previous example of producing social media content for real estate agents. A qualified lead would be a real estate agent who is in need of social media videos to advertise their services and is able to hire you. If a real estate agent doesn't have social media, would that be a qualified lead? Probably not.

What's an easier sell?

- Convincing a real estate agent that social media is a necessary advertising channel for their business, then convincing them to create social media channels for their business, then convincing them to hire you to capture content for them?

Or

- Convincing a real estate agent who is already active on social media but hasn't uploaded any video content to hire you?

Go for the easy sell; don't waste time trying to sell to those who aren't qualified.

Additionally, if a real estate agent is new to the industry and hasn't sold a home yet, is that a qualified lead? Probably not. They most likely do not have the budget to pay for your services if they don't yet have a solid business. They are probably more focused on outbound sales as opposed to building up their marketing efforts.

Does this mean it would be impossible to sell to them? No, but the goal here is to make the best use of your time when prospecting. Is it a better use of your time to spend all day cold calling real estate agents who have no sales yet or real estate agents with large marketing budgets? I would bet that you would make a lot more sales reaching out to real estate agents with large marketing budgets.

Outreach

Once you have a list of qualified leads, it's time to perform outreach. There are many different ways to effectively reach out to prospective clients, but the key is to find out what method works best for your *industry* and what method works best for *you*. Below are a few different avenues to perform outreach:

- In Person
- Cold Calling
- Email
- LinkedIn
- Instagram
- Facebook

Some prospecting methods work better for different industries. For example, when I ventured into real estate videography, I performed outreach to real estate agents to sell them on my services. I thought LinkedIn might be an effective route to perform outreach, so I found agents who had been in the industry for a number of years and began messaging them.

Days went by, and I wasn't hearing back from a large percentage of those I had messaged. Two weeks went by, and I started receiving messages from some I had contacted the first day. They told me that they did not check their LinkedIn often and to reach out to them directly either via email or their cell phone.

Through this, I discovered that real estate agents spend most of the day on their cell phones sending and receiving calls. They are reaching out to other agents on the phone for their clients or calling their clients to check in on them. I adjusted my outreach to cold calling and discovered that this was far more effective for the real estate niche.

Figure out what method of outreach is most effective for your niche.

You will also find that you are personally more effective at reaching out via some methods over others. Maybe going up to a business owner in person terrifies you, but you can cold email all day long.

Two things are true: You're not going to be effective at prospecting if you utilize an ineffective method for your industry, and you're not going to be effective at prospecting if you utilize a method that's ineffective for you.

If your target clients are not checking their email often, you can send emails all day long, but your efforts will be wasted. Show up where your prospects are. This could take time and testing. Utilize what you know about your target clients and the industry to determine where to start.

As I mentioned earlier, real estate agents are typically on their phone throughout the day. They are constantly checking in on clients over the phone and calling other agents to check in on their clients' listings or offers. For this reason, cold calling is a great prospecting method if you're in the real estate niche. Say you produce marketing videos for real estate agents or you specialize in creating real estate listing videos. Cold calling real estate agents would be a great prospecting method for you.

Now, what if you find that cold calling is not your strength? What if you dread the thought of spending all day calling clients? This might not be the method for you. For most niches there are multiple ways to effectively prospect. If being on the phone isn't your strength, try email outreach. If email outreach isn't your strength, try face-to-face interaction. If physically going to businesses isn't your strength, try social media outreach.

There are multiple ways to prospect, so find a route that's effective for your industry and effective for you. Now what if you're thinking, "None of those sound like fun to me." The simple fact is, prospecting can be one of the biggest drivers to growing your business and making money. You might not enjoy it right away, but it's important you stick with it. It will become more enjoyable over time as you master the process and see the sales rolling in.

Push through those nerves, make those calls, send those messages, and get in front of your target client. This is what will separate you from the average videographers. This is what will help you turn your camera into a six-figure videography business.

Once you connect with a client through prospecting, the goal is to spark interest in your services. You want to explain to them why they need your videos. In this step, utilize any data that you can to drive home your point. Numbers talk.

Whether you're reaching out over the phone, via email, or any other method, the structure of your message should follow this basic outline:

1. Greeting
2. Reason for Outreach
3. Pitch
4. Close

Greeting: Start with a polite greeting. It shouldn't be long, especially via written communication, but lead with some sort of greeting. This shows you're a person. People do business with people.

Reason for Outreach: Provide some sort of reason for your outreach. Don't jump directly into your pitch. Providing a reason for the outreach sets the stage for your pitch. This could be something along the lines of, "I came across your Instagram profile and love your content, but I noticed that you currently don't have any video content posted." Or, "I stumbled across your website, and I love the photos you have of your business, but I saw that you don't have a video on the homepage greeting website visitors."

Pitch: this is where you ignite the fire in them. This is where you get them to think, "Wow! I need to hear more about this." This is where you provide data to drive your point home. An example of this could look like, "Thank you for taking a few minutes to chat with me. As I mentioned, I noticed that your website does not have a video on the homepage to greet your website visitors. Studies show that sites that use video have a 4.8% conversion rate compared to 2.9% for sites without video.[11] That is almost double the conversions. Imagine if you were able to double the conversions for your business."

Close: You've greeted the prospect, shared why you are reaching out, and wowed them with how your videos could impact their business. Now it's time to close. You're not going to close the prospect with the first point of contact. Don't rush the sale. The goal here is to get the prospect interested enough to be able to schedule them for a presentation. The presentation is where you seal the deal.

For your close, you want to provide an alternative advance. An alternative advance is a common sales tactic used to move a prospect forward in the sales process. An alternative advance is when you provide a prospect with two options, both of which advance the sale. For example, "I would love to share options for how we can create videos for your website to help you increase conversions. I'm available Tuesday at 1 p.m. or Thursday at 3 p.m. Which time works best for you to jump on a Zoom call?" We'll talk about alternative advances throughout this book, but if you would like to learn more about alternative advances, I recommend reading *How to Master the Art of Selling* by Tom Hopkins.

Most videographers fall into the trap of "asking" themselves out of sales. In the example above, I have provided the prospect with two options in response to my question, with both options leading to another meeting. Most videographers would end the call by saying something similar to, "I would love to share options for how we can create videos for your website to help you increase conversions. Would you like to meet to learn more?"

In this scenario, the prospect is provided with two options, one of which is a way to terminate the sale. Don't "ask" yourself out of sales. Utilize alternative advances to advance the sales process. You might feel nervous the first time you use this tactic, but you will be amazed at how well it works and at how much higher your close rates become. Watch as your close rates increase drastically. This structure also works for all different types of outreach. You can use this structure for phone calls, emails, social media messaging, etc. You've effectively scheduled a time to deliver a presentation to the client, now you need to put together a killer presentation.

Presentation

You've identified your prospects, reached out, and effectively closed them on another meeting. Now it's time to move to the presentation stage of the sales process. The ultimate goal of the presentation is to provide the prospect with a convincing presentation that results in a sale. The structure for an effective presentation is as follows:

1. Rapport
2. Agenda
3. Mission
4. Package(s)
5. Close

Rapport: At the start of your meeting, lead by building rapport. Remember, people do business with people they like, know, and trust. Build that personal connection by creating rapport with the prospect at the start of your meeting. If your meeting is early in the week, ask how their weekend was. If the meeting is late in the week, ask if they have any fun plans in the coming weekend.

Find connections wherever possible and build positive rapport. Don't fall into the trap of jumping straight into the presentation. This can come off as "salesy." Once people feel like they are being sold to, they go on the defense. Foster the relationship, and build trust by leading with rapport.

Agenda: It's important to review the agenda for the meeting with the client. Provide them with a brief breakdown of what they can expect in the meeting. Once you have provided a breakdown of the meeting, remind them approximately how long the meeting will run until, and confirm that they are still available until that time. If they are not, be ready to provide the presentation in the given time frame. This section of the meeting can sound something like this:

> *I'm glad we were able to find time to connect today. I'm excited about the ways we can help you accomplish _____.*
> *Before we jump into it, I want to provide you with a brief agenda for our meeting, so you know what to expect.*
> *First, I will share a little bit more about how our video(s) can help you _____. Then I will provide you a breakdown of the different options I've put together for you and your business. In total, our meeting will probably run to around 1:30 p.m. Does that timeline still work for you?*

Mission: Once you've provided the prospect the agenda for the meeting and confirmed that they are still available until your scheduled time, it's time to move into the mission. The mission is where you drive home the realization for the client that they are in need of your video(s). This is where you want to once again utilize any data that you can to demonstrate the positive investment for the client. If you have any case studies, this is a great place to utilize those. I know it can be hard to come across data, and we don't always

139

have access to ROI for clients. If that is the case, utilize data that you can find from other trusted sources. Don't worry; I was able to build well over a six-figure videography business without having any extensive case studies or insider data for client ROI. You can do the same.

If you can't find data from trusted sources, then make an appeal to the client's emotions. Often, sales are made based on emotions as opposed to numbers. Make the client feel the benefits of your videos. If it's time that your videos will save for your client, make them feel the pain of the time that is wasted, and then make them feel the positive emotions of the time your videos will save them. If it's sales that your videos will help them earn, make them feel the pain of the lost sales, and then drive home the positive feeling of more money in their pockets from the sales your videos will help create.

Package(s): Once you've realigned on the mission, it's time to dive into the meat of the presentation. This is the part where you share the package or packages. You've set the stage. You've told them what the mission is. Now it's time to explain how you are going to help them achieve their goals. There are a few strategies that you can utilize when presenting options to the client. Below are some of these strategies:

- **Good-Better-Best Pricing:** This strategy helps the client feel like they are in the driver's seat by empowering them with options. With good-better-best pricing you provide the client with three packages to choose from across three levels of features and three levels of price points. In addition to empowering the client to select the package of their choice, they additionally have the ability to select a more affordable option if their budget does not allow for the more expensive options. This can result in more closed sales.

- **Delayed Pricing:** This strategy focuses on waiting to share prices until you have adequately shared the value your video(s) will bring the client. Sharing prices too early in the sales process can cause you to lose the client's attention. They will be focused on the price while you're talking about the details of the packages. If you share the price before you share the value, you will have to justify the price to the client. At this point, you've already lost. You want to keep the prospect's focus on the benefits and breakdown of the package before sharing the price.

- **Price Anchoring:** This is a handy sales technique that is as old as time. In its simplest form, price anchoring is the technique of presenting the client with the option that requires the largest investment first and continuing in descending order. When the client sees the initial cost of the most expensive option, the prices for the other options appear more affordable. If you are presenting multiple options to the client, which I recommend in most cases, then utilize this strategy.

- **Charm Prices:** This sales technique is used everywhere you look. Make your prices appear more affordable by pricing them just under a round figure. For example, say I was going to price a video package at $3,500. Instead of setting $3,500 as the price, I would drop it just below. While it might only be the difference of a few dollars, it can help the overall price appear significantly more affordable. I additionally like to end my packages with a "70." If you price all of your packages ending at "99," it can appear gimmicky to the client. I have found ending prices in a "70" feels like more thought was put into the pricing point, and it still allows you to drop the price below a round figure. Using the example above, I would price the package at $3,470.

- **Remove Commas:** removing commas is helpful in making your price appear less daunting. The more characters you have added onto a price, the more expensive it appears to the eye. For example, let's say you were pricing a video package at $4,970. What is the dollar difference between $4970 and $4,970.00? None. But the added comma, decimal point, and extra zeros makes the price figure appear more intimidating. Drop unnecessary figures in your pricing.

Close: Once you have walked the client through the package(s), it's time to close. Ideally, you are able to close on the spot. If the individual you are meeting with is the ultimate decision maker, push to try and close at the end of your meeting. Use the three-question close:

1. Which package most aligns with your vision for this project?
2. I know you're looking to get these videos out by <date #1>. I'm available to meet on the <date #2> at <time #1> or the <date #2> at <time #2> to start the planning phase for the video(s). Which time works best for you?
3. I will send over the invoice for the first half of the project. What is the best email to send that to?

Asking "Which package most aligns with your vision for this project?" when offering multiple packages does two things:

1. If the client likes a certain package, this question leads them to tell you which package they like most.
2. If the client has hesitations about the packages, this question leads them to share that with you.

If you were able to provide a strong enough case for why the client needs your video(s) in the start of the meeting, the client is likely to share with you which package is catching their eye. When they tell you this, lead into Question 2: "Great! I know you're looking to get these videos out by <date>. I'm available to meet on the <date #1> at <time #1> or the <date #2> at <time #2> to start the planning phase for the video(s). Which time works best for you?"

Once they answer this question, it's time to seal the deal. At that point, say, "I will send over the invoice for the first half of the project. What is the best email to send that to?" Once they provide you the best person to send the invoice to, you're good as gold. Remember, it's not your job to talk yourself out of a sale. You should be confident in the product that you're producing for the client. Don't ask questions like, "Would you like to move forward with this package?" After you look at the menu at a restaurant, does the waiter ask you, "Would you like to order any food?" No. The assumption is that you are there to eat. The question is, "What would you like to eat?" You have the power to create videos that your client needs. Assume that your client is there to purchase. Use alternative advance questions to close more deals, and utilize the three-question close to get the job done.

Once you master the art of outbound sales, you will see your income soar. At the end of the day, you're only going to close a percentage of the prospects you reach out to. Don't become discouraged. Utilize the strategies I have shared in this chapter to increase the percentage of clients you are closing and from there, it becomes a numbers game. Keep reaching out to qualified leads and you will continue closing sales.

Now that we've reviewed the first phase of the 3-Phase Approach to 6-Figure Sales—outbound sales—let's talk about the second phase—inbound sales.

Chapter 17
INBOUND SALES

What are inbound sales? Inbound sales are the sales that come knocking on your door, saying, "Hey! I am interested in utilizing your videography services." Inbound sales start with an inbound lead. An Inbound lead is a prospective client who reaches out to you inquiring about your videography services.

What do inbound leads look like? Inbound leads can come in a variety of ways, but some of the most common are:

- a submission of a contact form through your website
- a phone call
- an email
- a text message
- a DM on social media

These leads typically reach out via one of the above contact methods because they become aware of your services through a referral or via your marketing materials. When I first started my videography business, my inbound sales process was a mess. My inbound sales "process" looked like the following:

- I receive an email from a prospect who was referred to me by someone I know. The prospect saw a video I created for my past client and is interested in using video for their business.

- I read through the email 10 times, trying to figure out what I should do next. What type of video does this prospect want? What is their budget? Where do I go from here?

- I spend two days stuck in analysis paralysis.

- On the third day I send the prospect a lengthy email asking for more information about the prospective client's "vision" for utilizing video content for their business.

- *Crickets.*

- I think about reaching back out, but I'm too nervous to send a follow-up email right away. I say I'll do it later. Later never comes … Lost sale.

It took me time and a lot of lost opportunities to create a process that has allowed me to tackle inbound sales with confidence, effectiveness, and speed. My hope is that the process I outline in this chapter allows you to feel confident on knowing steps to take next time you get that inbound lead in your inbox or that DM on social media from someone who's interested in your services.

Let's go ahead and break down the three stages of an inbound sale:

1. Point of Interest
2. Understanding Needs
3. Providing Solutions

Point of Interest

The first step to securing a sale is getting the prospective client interested in your services. You cannot land a sale without getting a client interested in your services. You also cannot get a client interested in your services if they are unaware of your services. This is why the point of interest can be further broken down into three distinct steps:

1. Initial Contact
2. Lead Research
3. Securing Meeting

Initial Contact: This is the moment that a prospective client becomes aware of your services. Remember, people do business with people they know, like, and trust. The first part of the equation is for people to know about your business. You could be capable of producing the best videos your niche has ever seen, but if nobody knows about your company, you won't make any sales.

When it comes to inbound sales, most clients will become aware of your services through word of mouth or your marketing materials. We will touch more on how to create an effective stream of word-of-mouth clients later in this chapter, so for now, we will focus on effective marketing.

Marketing is a great way to create passive inbound leads for your business. Many forms of marketing can work for you day and night advertising your business while you focus on other areas of your business. What are some great opportunities to secure inbound leads through marketing?

Methods to Secure Inbound Leads

Social media is a fantastic platform to market your business. As of the time of this writing, there are an estimated 4.76 billion (with a 'B') active users on social media and the average user spends two hours and 31 minutes per day on social media.[12] That means on average, 59.4% of the world's population is spending 2.5 hours on social media every day. And guess what? That is a free opportunity for you to market your business to prospective clients.

It's no secret that social media changes all of the time, but don't fall prey to thinking that you have to spend every waking hour of your day trying to "crack the code" on the latest way to go viral on social media. The simple fact is that you don't need millions of followers on social media to earn very real dollars for your business. You don't even need thousands of followers.

When I did wedding videography part-time at the start of my videography career, I decided to create an Instagram account for my wedding videography business. I made a commitment to posting three times a week for two months. At the time, I had only filmed around five weddings, so most of the content I was posting was small clips from the weddings I had shot or screenshots of some of my favorite shots I had captured throughout those wedding days.

I started with around 100 followers on the Instagram account at the start of the two months and ended the two months with around 233 followers on the Instagram account. Not much, right? With those 233 followers on that Instagram account, I booked $50,000 worth of wedding videography clients that year.

You don't need tens of thousands of followers and hundreds of thousands of views to make tens of thousands of dollars from marketing your business on social media. Take advantage of this free avenue to marketing your business, and don't fall prey to the false information people are out there pedaling, saying that marketing your business on social media is dead or that you have to go viral in order to grow your business on social media. Most of those people are either too lazy to put in the effort to post consistently, or they're trying to sell you something.

When marketing your business on social media, focus on a few things:

1. Utilize the platform that your customers spend time on.

    Don't try to market to corporate executives on Instagram. If you're targeting corporate decision makers, you will probably have better success on LinkedIn. Find out what platform your target prospects are on, and market your business on that platform.

2. Show up consistently.

    Don't expect to post one piece of content on social media and have clients flooding your inbox. It could happen, but it's not likely. The key with social media is to be consistent. Posting three days a week is great, but pick the right cadence that you will be able to maintain consistently month over month. If you can do more, even better. If you can only manage one time a week, do it.

3. Engage with people.

    Too many people waste time passively on social media. You jump on Instagram, scroll through your feed, read things, watch things, and exit the app. Mindless scrolling will not help you grow your business. Every time you get on social media, you should be engaging with your prospects. Follow a few of your target clients on the platform of your choosing, then each time you get on, engage with their content. "Like" their posts, comment on their posts, and DM them valuable content. This engagement will foster relationships that turn into inbound leads.

Build an Effective Website: Your website should act as a 24-hour salesperson. Search engines, such as Google, have a mission of connecting online traffic to the websites they are looking for. People understand the need for video in their businesses and in their lives. For this reason, many people are actively seeking out businesses that can help them meet their videography needs.

Set up your website so when Google sends someone to it, they are converting into inbound leads. You're probably not going to be receiving a new contact form every day from your website (depending on your niche and the money you are spending toward SEO), but one contact form per quarter from a client with a $5,000 budget could mean $20,000 in additional income if your website is set up effectively.

To set up your website in a manner that directs people to inquire about your services, focus on the following:

1. All of your website content should have the end goal of leading visitors to submitting a contact form.

a. Create a video for the homepage of your website that tells your visitors who you are, how you can help them, and where to submit a contact form.

b. Create a strong "Work" page that showcases some of your best work. This is where your portfolio should live. When visitors see this page, they should think to themselves, "I need these same videos for my business!"

c. Create a "Contact Us" page on your website that is visually appealing and easy to fill out. You should then have a button linking to this page in the top right corner of every page of your website. Pro tip: Include a testimonial from a former client on this page. Testimonials are proven to increase conversion rates on contact forms.

Join Community Groups: There are numerous community groups out there that are created to help businesses connect with the community and other businesses in the community. One of the most popular in the US is the Chamber of Commerce. Most cities have a local Chamber of Commerce. These groups are a great way to connect with prospects and grow your business.

Many of these organizations have listings where they will put your business information. That way any other members of the organization can search for "videography," "video production," or similar keywords and your business will pop up.

As I mentioned earlier in the book, I joined my local Chamber of Commerce in my first full year in my business. Joining the organization led to $4,800 worth of work within the first six months. This has grown to much larger amounts over time as I have continued to develop relationships through the organization. A tip for anybody getting started who is looking for free ways to market their business: Oftentimes these organizations have yearly fees. For example, the annual fee when I joined my local Chamber of Commerce was $300; however, as already mentioned, after a few days in the group, one of the marketing coordinators in the chamber asked if I would be willing to shoot a video for them in exchange for waiving my fees along with an array of different advertising opportunities through their organization.

If you're interested in joining a group like your local Chamber of Commerce, but you don't want to spend any money to join, offer to create a video for them in exchange for waiving your fees. This will save you money, show your work to a great group of connected people, and provide you with a new portfolio piece.

Once you've created your marketing materials to get your business in front of your prospects, over time, inbound leads will start to come in. Now comes the question, what should you do once you receive an inbound lead? The next step depends on the form of the inbound lead.

Book a Discovery Call

Did the lead come in through a method where the client provided their phone number? This is oftentimes through a website contact form, a text, or a phone call. If yes, then it's time to move straight to the Discovery Call section of this chapter. A discovery call is a phone call where you ask the client questions that provide you with the knowledge you need to create video packages for them.

Research the client to create your discovery questions, and then give the client a call. Once you have the client on the phone, ask if they have time to answer a few questions in regards to their inquiry. If they say yes, proceed with your discovery call. If they do not, set a time to meet for the call at a later date. Skip ahead to the Discovery Call portion of this chapter for more information.

If the client reaches out via a method where their phone number is not provided, the goal is to get a discovery call booked with the prospect. Trust is built over the phone, not via email or messaging. From here, message them back using the following structure:

- Thank them for reaching out.
- Demonstrate excitement and proficiency in regards to their needs.
- Offer times to meet for a phone call.

An example of a message could be:

Hi, Joe. Thank you for considering us for your video needs. We would love the opportunity to assist you with your needs in regards to _____. We're also happy to say we have plenty of experience in this area as we have helped _____ in the past with a similar project.

From here, I would like to gain a deeper understanding of exactly what type of video content would be most beneficial to you and your business. The best way for us to do this is to jump on a quick 30-minute phone call. I'm available <date #1> at <time #1> and <date #2> at <time #2>. Which of those times works best for you?

Once the prospect comes back with the best time for them, send them a calendar invite to lock the meeting in on their calendar. Now that you've set your discovery call with the client, it's time to move to the next stage of the inbound sales process, understanding needs.

Understanding Needs

This is an area many videographers go astray, and the reason is that most videographers have no formal training in sales. I hope this book equips you with the sales strategy, process, and tactics that you need to book more business. Before you are able to lock in a client for a project, you must have an understanding of what the project is that you'll be completing for the client. It sounds so simple, but many times videographers don't ask the right questions that will enable them to offer the right video that solves the client's problems. The goal of this stage is to understand your client's needs. Once you know your client's needs, you can provide the video that will solve those problems. This phase is broken into two parts: the research and the discovery call. Let's look first at the research.

The Research

The key to landing a deal is being able to diagnose the client's problem so that you can prescribe the right solution. When I was prepping for the discovery call for what ultimately became my first five-figure deal, I did a deep-dive on the company, their industry, and their marketing channels. Based on the email I had received from them indicating interest in my services, I knew that they were looking for video content for their website and social media channels.

I scrolled through each page of their website identifying areas that could be improved with the integration of video. I scrolled through months of their social media feeds taking screenshots analyzing what type of posts performed well, what type of posts performed poorly, and what type of posts could help increase their engagement. Through my research, I knew key terms from their industry, I knew the state of their current marketing efforts, and I was able to put together informed questions for our discovery call to help me create the perfect packages for the client.

The goal of the research phase is to have the knowledge necessary to ask the questions necessary to understand the client's challenges, the client's goals, and how you can help them bridge the gap between the two.

You're not looking to prescribe the solution in your initial meeting as the client reached out for a reason and likely has thoughts that they want to share. You just want to know the questions you need to ask to extract the right information from the client. What does research look like? Use the information provided in the initial contact from the client to inform what type of research you should be doing. If the client mentions wanting to bolster their website, become familiar with their website. If the client is looking for video content for their social media, check out all of their social media channels. If the client mentions wanting video content similar to another business, research the other business to see what type of content they are posting.

Once you've done the research, you will be able to create a list of the questions necessary to learn the client's challenges, goals, and how you can bridge the gap between the two. You find out the answers to these questions in the next step, the discovery call.

The Discovery Call

You've done the research to create your list of questions to ask, and now it's time to move to the discovery call. The discovery call is where you gain a full understanding of the client's problems so that you can put together the solutions that will solve those problems. A discovery call is best suited to a phone call.

A phone call provides a low-level of commitment to a prospective client but at the same time allows you to build trust. A discovery call can also happen via another method such as a video call or in person, but I've found that you're more likely to receive a commitment from a new client if you offer a lower-level commitment in the form of a phone call.

A successful discovery call can be broken into three steps:

1. Preparation
2. Discovery
3. Scheduling

Preparation

Preparation starts by creating the list of questions you will ask the client on your call. Use the research you performed in the previous phase along with the contents of the client's initial outreach to create your list of questions. Ask questions that are important for understanding the client's challenges, their needs, and how you can help them. Don't fall into the trap of asking questions to ask questions. Your questions should be intentional and necessary.

Once you have your list of questions, it's time to create your agenda for the call. A basic agenda for discovery calls is as follows:

1. Building Rapport
2. Sharing the Agenda
3. Asking Questions
4. Scheduling Your Next Meeting

Building Rapport: You've heard me say it once, you've heard me say it twice, and you'll hear me say it a hundred more times by the end of this book—people do business with people they like, know, and trust. Likeability and trust are built in small moments when you're having casual conversation, like at the start of a meeting. Don't come out hot at the start of your meeting, guns blazing, fixed on talking business, unless you sense that's what the client wants.

Use that time to build rapport with the client and build that foundation of likeability and trust. How do you do this? Show genuine interest in the client on a personal level. Remember, we view sales as a partnership. Treat people like people, and your business will thrive. Here are some great questions to ask to build rapport at the start of your meeting:

- How is your week going?
- How has your day been?
- Did you do anything fun this weekend?
- I saw that your team did _____ the other day! How was that?

These are just a few ideas to get you thinking. When asking questions, try to get the client to talk about things that will be positive and foster connection. Anytime you have the opportunity to discuss commonalities, you are building trust and forming a relationship. "You went to ___ this weekend? I love that place! What did you think of ____?" "You watched ___ this weekend? That is such a great movie! What did you think of ____?"

Lastly, tailor your rapport to the client. Try to get a sense for the client's likes and dislikes. Talk about the things they enjoy, and avoid the things they don't. Listen more than you talk, and you will be well on your way to building trust at the start of your meeting.

Sharing the Agenda: Once you've initiated the meeting with pleasantries and built positive rapport, it's time to move to the agenda. Sharing the agenda sets expectations for the client, makes them comfortable, and makes it easier for both of you to accomplish the goals of the meeting. An example of sharing a meeting agenda is, "My hope with our time today is to figure out what challenges you're currently facing in your business and to see if we can solve those problems with the use of video." Notice the language here? The structure of this sentence positions you as a partner, not an imposer. Partners seek to understand needs, imposers wish to force their services onto someone.

Steer clear of using phrases similar to, "My goal for today is to figure out ways we can integrate video into your business." See the difference? This language portrays you as somebody who is trying to force a square peg into a round hole. This is the language of somebody who is hunting for a sale, not somebody who is looking to partner with a client. Your goal should not be to weasel your videos into a business's budget. Your goal should be to figure out what your client's needs are and determine if you are able to solve those needs with your services.

Asking Questions: Once you've shared the agenda with the client, it's time to get into the meat of the discovery meeting. It's time to ask questions. Remember, the goal here is to ask the questions that will identify the client's challenges and help you understand the type of videos that will solve those challenges for the client. With the research you performed before your call and the items the client mentioned in their initial contact, you already have a head start. Both of these should inform the questions that you are asking during this portion of the discovery meeting.

The experienced videographer says, "I saw that you want to leverage your website better. Tell me more about that." The client responds with, "We are getting a lot of traffic to our contact form, but we aren't receiving the number of submissions we would like." Now you know the full-picture and start to see the solution to the problem. Through your research, you know that the client does not have a video on their contact form. You should create a video to place on the same page as the contact form to showcase the benefits of the client's product or service.

You say to the client, "Video is a high-converting form of media that can improve conversion rates for contact forms. I think adding a video to the same page as your contact form could be a way for us to increase submissions. Is that something that you would be interested in?"

When asking questions during the discovery meeting, below are a few keys to focus on:

- Utilize the prior research you performed to direct the questions that you ask.
- Ask questions that help you understand the client's business.
- Ask questions that help you understand the client's challenges.
- Ask questions that help you form solutions for the client's challenges.
- Ask questions that help you understand the consequences of your client's needs not being met.
- Ask questions that help you understand the client's constraints.
- Ultimately, you want to ask the questions that provide you the information that you need to create packages for your client.

Scheduling the Next Meeting: Now that you have all of the information you need to create packages for your client, it's time to finish the meeting by locking your next meeting in on the calendar. Why do this before ending the meeting? You have a captive audience. You have the client's full attention when you are speaking with them. Setting a time for the next meeting before you end the call ensures that you get that meeting on the calendar. Once it's on the calendar, it's likely to happen.

Those who wait to schedule the next meeting press the pause button on the sales process. The meeting has ended, and there is no follow-up action. The sales process stalls out, you email the client the next day providing them options for the next meeting. They open the email between meetings and decide they'll get back to it later.

An issue pops up in the client's business that they must take immediate action on. Your email falls to the back of their mind. A few days go by, and the client remembers they have yet to schedule that next meeting. They question whether video is something they need to focus on right now. They decide they have other items to prioritize. Lost sale.

Don't let this happen. Before you end your meeting, get the next meeting scheduled. This drastically increases the odds of the meeting happening and the odds of you closing the sale. How do you go about getting the next meeting scheduled before the end of the call? If you have done a good job of building rapport and asking the right questions, the client is likely to want to meet with you again. After you have asked all of your questions, say something similar to:

> *It was great meeting with you today and learning more about your business. I feel confident that I can produce the type of video(s) that will allow you to accomplish _____. I'm going to put together a few options for us to review during our next meeting. I'm available tomorrow*

from 3 p.m. to 4 p.m. or Thursday from 1 p.m. to 2 p.m.
What time works best for you?

Start by showing gratitude for your client's time. Follow up by informing the client that you are confident that you are able to provide the type of video(s) that will help them achieve their goals or overcome their challenges. Inform them that you are going to put together options for them to review during your next meeting and provide times that you are available to meet. This is important. Don't say, "When would be the best time for us to meet next?" This type of question is more likely to be met with, "I'm pretty booked up through the rest of the week. Go ahead and email me the packages, and I'll review them."

Provide them with times and they are likely to look at their calendar to check those times. If they are actually booked during those times, they will likely say, "I'm sorry I'm booked up at both of those times. How about Wednesday at 4 p.m.?" Why is this? You've set the expectation that you are planning another meeting. If they don't provide an alternative time, say something such as, "Not a problem. I am also available tomorrow from 4 p.m. to 5 p.m., Friday from 12 p.m. to 1 p.m., and Monday from 1 p.m. to 2 p.m. Which of those times works best for you?"

Provide them with two options the first time you ask. Don't overwhelm the client. If you provide them with more than two options, they will likely become overwhelmed and find it easier to ask you to send over the options via email so they can review. Confused people don't buy. You're selling the prospect on another meeting; don't overwhelm them with too many meeting times. If they aren't able to make either of the two times, then you can offer three new options. By this point, they are more deeply committed and more likely to make one of those times work.

The goal is to get the next meeting scheduled for a date and time that is in the near future. You don't want to offer times that are two weeks out. Every additional day that goes by is more time that they can lose interest in moving forward with your services or something can affect their budget to no longer make video a priority. Try to get the follow-up meeting scheduled for a time within the next week, ideally within two to five days.

What do you do if you offer times to meet and the client says, "I'm pretty booked up over the next few days. Can you just send me the options via PDF so that I can review them on my own?" Hopefully, by this point, you will have built enough trust with the client that they will be excited to meet with you again to hear about the options you have put together, but if not, there are still ways to handle this.

If this happens, put the benefits back on the client. Say, "You will likely have questions as we go through the packages, and I don't want you to have to hassle with trying to send all of your questions via email. I can save you time and just answer them for you on the spot. Meeting over a video call will also allow me to make any adjustments to the packages that you would like so that we can create the perfect video to solve your challenges. We can meet Wednesday at 4 p.m., or would Thursday at 2 p.m work better for your schedule?"

See how the benefit to the client is at the forefront of this response? Meeting over a video call will save the client time and allow you to better serve their needs. What's not to love? Lastly, you should once again finish with an alternative advance. Provide them options for times, and ask what time works best for them. Don't finish with your statement of benefits. That allows them to come back with another objection. Finish by providing meeting times, asking which of the times works best for them, and you're leading them toward the response that you're shooting for.

If the client comes back again asking you to send them a PDF with the packages, don't fight it. They have either lost interest in utilizing your services, or they are truly too busy to meet with you. In either case, put together packages and email them over. I've still closed sales even when the client is too busy for me to present the options. The odds aren't as high that the client is going to move forward with the sales process, but it's still worth one last Hail Mary attempt. Email the packages to the client, and ask what option is most appealing to them.

Providing Solutions

Now comes the final stage in earning business through inbound sales. You created the point of interest through marketing efforts, you gained an understanding of your client's needs through your discovery call, now it's time to provide solutions to earn the sale. This stage of the inbound sales process is going to be very similar to the "provide solutions" stage of the outbound sales process that we reviewed in the last chapter.

For this reason, I will touch lightly on some of the points we discussed in the previous chapter. If you would like more context around certain topics, revisit the Provide Solutions section of the last chapter on outbound sales. This stage of the inbound sales process can be broken down into three unique steps:

1. Create Packages
2. Create Presentation
3. Deliver Presentation

Create Packages: The first step to closing the sale is offering a video that is going to be irresistible to the client. In order to do this, you must take all of the information that you have about your client's business, their challenges, and put together a solution. Utilize the topics they touched on within their initial outreach, utilize the research you did prior to reaching out to them, and utilize the notes you took during your discovery call. By this point, you should have a clear understanding of your client's business, their goals, their challenges, and what type of video(s) will help them overcome their challenges and accomplish their goals.

You might have noticed that I have stated, "Create packages" plural. When working through the sales process, it is often most advantageous to create multiple packages for the client. I mentioned this in the previous chapter on outbound sales, but let's take a deeper look into the advantages of offering the client options. Offering multiple options accomplishes a few different things:

1. It strengthens the feeling of partnership between you and the client.
2. It allows the client to make decisions based on their budget.
3. It opens you up to more potential revenue.

It strengthens the feeling of partnership between you and the client. When clients are provided only one solution to their problem, it can feel like they are being "spoken at" instead of "partnered with." One option indicates, "It's this or nothing." It's a yes or a no. Remember, everything in the sales process should be focused on partnership. By providing a client with three ways to accomplish the same goal, you are creating partnership. You are opening the door for dialogue. You have a conversation about the differences between the packages and find out exactly which one is right for them.

It allows the client to make decisions based on their budget. Hopefully by this point, you have an idea of what the client's budget is, but you might not know exactly what that number is. By providing options, you are offering the client the opportunity to buy across a number of price points which increases your potential to close the sale. Utilize your knowledge of what the project will cost you to produce based on your time, equipment use, and any help you'll have to hire. Combine that with your knowledge of what value the end product will provide to your client along with their budgetary constraints.

Use all of this information to create a "base option." From there, add additional items that can further improve the video and use these items to create two more packages that are at a higher price point. The client might only have enough of a budget to afford the base package, but if the budget allows for it, they have the option to move forward with the other more expensive options. This puts them in the driver's seat and makes them feel like they are being partnered with and not sold to.

It opens you up to more revenue. By providing options, you are also opening yourself up to making more money. If you only offer the client one option, you're either making that amount of money, or you're walking away with nothing. When you offer multiple options, you're allowing the client to select a higher-priced option if they so choose. Oftentimes marketers will have a set amount of budget that they can put toward a certain project. If they have the option to spend more on a cleaner, more well-polished video, they might want that option. Don't prevent them from making that decision by offering a single option.

I once had a business reach out looking for assistance capturing a conference that they were in charge of organizing. They wanted a highlight video showcasing how much fun the conference was and all of the educational benefits it provided to its attendees. I figured out my base package using the information that I had received from the initial contact, my research of the business, and the answers to my questions on the discovery call. The base package was one day of shooting and two days of editing and required basic audio gear, a single camera, a few lenses, and a stabilizer. I quoted the base package at $2,970. (Notice that charm pricing.) I knew that I could create an even better video if I brought along some extra equipment, so I added two additional options for the client. One was at $4,700 and the other was at $7,400. The client ended up booking me for $7,400.

These are the benefits of creating options for your client as opposed to offering a single video option. With all of this being said, make decisions based on your experience with the client as well as your unique situation. If it's clear that the client only wants one option, provide one option. I've found that three is often the best number of options. Three provides the client with choices without overwhelming them. If you offer more than three options, you risk overwhelming the client, which can result in the sale falling through. This is known as decision fatigue.

A famous study conducted by Sheena S. Iyengar of Columbia University and Mark R. Lepper of Stanford University discovered that customers were almost eight times more likely to make a purchasing decision when presented with six purchasing options compared to 24.[13] This study was conducted with a simple product, jam. With something as intricate as videography services, I've found that three is the sweet spot for the number of options to provide the client. This gives the client choices without overwhelming them and creating decision fatigue.

When creating packages for the client, utilize the other strategies that we reviewed in Chapter 17. Review the below strategies from Chapter 17 if you need to:

- Good-Better-Best Pricing
- Delayed Pricing
- Price Anchoring
- Charm Prices
- Remove Unnecessary Figures

Now that you have your packages created, let's talk about the setup for your phase three meeting. This meeting is best completed either in person or on a video call. Clients are more invested in meetings the more physically present they are in the meeting as we discussed in the last chapter.

If the client pushes back on meeting either in person or on a video call, outline that it is necessary that the client be able to visually see the packages along with examples that you will provide during your meeting. You can say something along the lines of, "Meeting over a video call will allow me to show you some visuals that will help better display the different options we will be reviewing. I can meet tomorrow at 4 p.m. for a video call. Or would Thursday at 2 p.m. work better for you?"

Now it's time to structure your meeting. The meeting should be structured as follows:

1. Rapport
2. Agenda
3. Review Challenges
4. Presentation of Solutions
5. Close

Rapport: Similar to the discovery call, you want to begin the meeting with rapport. Have casual conversation that allows the client to decompress and feel comfortable in the meeting space. A few great ways to do this are by:

- Asking how their day is going
- Asking how their week is going
- Reconnecting on a non-business-related topic that you discussed in your last meeting

Reconnecting on a non-business-related topic that you discussed in your previous meeting can be one of the strongest ways to build rapport. This builds trust by sharing common dialogue and additionally shows that you are truly listening to the client. If you weren't listening, then you wouldn't have remembered what they shared about their personal lives in your discovery call.

Agenda: Once you've built rapport, transition to the agenda. Sharing the agenda further builds comfort for the client. People are uncomfortable when they are left in the unknown. By reviewing the agenda, you are providing them an outline for how you will spend your time together. They will find comfort in knowing what to expect through each stage of the meeting. You can say something along the lines of, "I'm excited to talk to you about the different options that I put together to solve ___. To provide context as to how we'll spend our time together today, first, we'll review some of the items we discussed last week in regards to ___. Then, we'll talk about the different options that I created for ___."

After outlining the agenda, you should finish by sharing how long the client can expect the meeting to last. This ensures that you will have their undivided attention throughout the entire meeting. You don't want the client to anticipate the meeting lasting 30 minutes less than what you planned for. This results in a distracted client trying to manage multiple priorities at once or the client cutting you off midway through the meeting, letting you know that you will need to finish at another time.

A good way to go about this is by saying, "The meeting should last around ___ total. Does that still work for your schedule?" If they say yes, great! If they say they need to be done in a certain amount of time, then you know to spend time on the most important parts and remove items where necessary.

Review Challenges: Now that you've laid out the agenda, it's time to move to reviewing the challenges. The goal with reviewing the client's challenges is to place the client into a state of mind where their challenges are top of mind. You want the client to feel the pain they feel when they are experiencing the challenges.

That will make the payoff more rewarding when you present the options that will help them overcome these challenges. You can say something similar to, "On our last call, we talked about how your most immediate business goals were _____. You shared how _____ was a significant challenge to overcoming these goals. Does that all line up with what you're still experiencing?"

Notice the structure of these sentences. You start by reviewing the goals they shared on the discovery call. You then outline the challenges they discussed that were preventing them from achieving those goals. From there, you ask if they are still experiencing those same challenges. You are teeing yourself up to hit a homerun. 99 times out of 100, as long as you asked the right questions and listened properly during the discovery call, the client is going to say, "Yes, that is exactly what we are experiencing." You have now confirmed that the packages that you've put together are geared toward solving their immediate problems, and more importantly, they have also verbally confirmed this. Every verbal confirmation from the client brings you one step closer to closing the deal.

Presentation of Solutions: Now that you've confirmed with the client that they are in need of a solution for the challenges you reviewed, it's time to present the solution(s). Every presentation is going to be different based on the industry and your client's needs, but a good rule of thumb is to keep your presentation between 14 and 18 minutes. This is long enough to provide a thorough presentation, but short enough to maintain your client's attention. Shorter than 14 minutes and you might find it tough to adequately outline the presentation. Longer than 18 minutes, and you greatly risk losing your client's attention and losing the sale.

This ideal range was discovered by TED Talks, the world's foremost authority in delivering powerful presentations.[14] TED requires all of their presenters to deliver their presentations in under 18 minutes, everyone from Simon Sinek to the Pope.

Most importantly, you want to make the client confident that your video(s) are the solution to their problems. Utilize all of the information that you have gathered so far to create a killer sales pitch. Utilize case studies, testimonials, and industry data to help strengthen your pitch. For example, let's say that you're presenting options to produce video content for a client's social media pages. You can say something like, "I have put together three options for boosting your reach via social media with the integration of video. Studies show that utilizing video on social media can increase your reach by ____. With these three options, I feel confident that we can help you increase your reach." You might not be able to guarantee results, but effective sales involves utilizing data to showcase historical results so that you can paint a picture of what future outcomes might look like.

As you break down the different options for the client, pause to ask them questions throughout. Your presentation should not be a monologue. Keep the client engaged by asking them questions. When possible, ask questions that lead them to confirm things they like about the packages. You can say something like, "I know on our previous call, you had mentioned that it was important to you to showcase shots of people physically using the product. With this option, we will be able to showcase five different people using the product in three different locations. Does that sound like something you would like?"

Given the client had previously mentioned this was something important to them, you can be confident that they are going to say yes. That yes is subconsciously telling them, "This is the perfect video for our goals." Do this as much as you can throughout the presentation while keeping it natural. Every small yes is bringing you a step closer to the final yes that closes the sale.

Close: Once you are finished presenting the options, it's time to close. Most videographers go astray in this area by thinking it's not possible to close a sale in the meeting. Not only is it possible, it's probable if you've been able to execute on all of the steps up to this point. Closing is an art, and it's important that you approach it with the right strategy. Once you've presented the client with the options, and they have presented no further questions, proceed with your closing question.

A favorite of mine is to use the three questions we discussed in the previous chapter on outbound sales. I start by asking, "It sounds like package ___ is the best fit for you. Do you agree?" After your presentation and dialogue, you should have an understanding of which package the client is leaning toward. Once the client responds with yes, come back with the second question, "Great! I know you're looking to get these videos out next month. I'm available to shoot on the fifth or the fifteenth. Which date works best for your schedule?" Once they provide their preferred shoot date, follow with the third and final question, "Great! I will add that to my calendar. What is the best email to send the deposit for the project to?" Once they answer this question, the deal is good as closed. Send over a calendar invite for the project along with the invoice for the deposit.

Don't ask, "Would you like to move forward with the project?" You've partnered with them to identify the right video to solve their problems. If you're confident in your services, the only questions left should be logistics around moving forward with the project, not whether or not they want to move forward with the project. This should not feel "salesy" if you've asked the right questions to understand their needs, taken the time to put together packages that will likely solve those needs, and partnered with them to identify which of the packages was best for them. It's not your job to place doubt in the client's mind.

Do the right thing, and do the necessary work during the "understanding needs" stage and "creating packages" stage so that you can close with confidence during your presentation.

If the client comes back with, "I would like to give this some more time to consider before moving forward," then work to identify what areas are causing them to pause. Maybe there was a certain subject that you did not outline with as much detail as you intended. Or maybe there was a challenge that the client did not mention during your discovery call that they would like to address.

Say to the client, "Of course, I want you to make sure package ___ is the right package for you. So I can save you time in reaching back out with additional questions? What area would you like to think through further?" Don't assume the answer is always money. Oftentimes, the financial investment will be the hurdle preventing them from moving forward with the project, but this is not always the case, and you don't want to insult the client by saying, "I know this is a big financial investment, but ___, ____, and ____ are why this will make you more money in the long run." The challenge could be something else entirely, and it looks silly if you were to assume that it all comes down to money.

By leading with the former question, you are demonstrating care and curiosity. You care because you want to save the client time and answer any questions they might have, and your curiosity comes across as a desire to find the right solution for the client. This question will most often lead the client to share what their hesitation is. This provides you an opportunity to overcome that challenge by reiterating the benefits that the client will experience with the video(s) or making adjustments to the packages if necessary.

For example, let's say that the client is hesitant because of the cost of the video(s). Take the time to lean into the hesitation. Ask questions that help you understand their hesitation. Remember, this is a partnership. In response, you can say, "Tell me more, is your concern the financial investment of the deposit or the financial investment of the entire project?" This will likely prompt the client to share more details about why budget is a challenge.

Once you have all of the details, restate the concern to the client to ensure that you are on the same page. If budget is a concern, you can say, "It sounds like your budget for this quarter has already been allocated toward other areas, and that does not include this project. Is that correct?" At this point, the client will likely confirm that you are correct. You are now on a level playing field.

At this point, you have taken the time to understand their concerns and listened to them so that you fully understand their hesitations. Proceed by adjusting the package to overcome their concerns if possible. If that is not possible, reiterate the most important benefits of the package to the client.

In the previous example, to adjust the package to meet the client's needs you could say, "It's completely understandable that this project was not originally included in your budgeting for this quarter. It sounds like this project would have an immediate effect on your team's budget. With that being said, I'm confident that you will be pleased with the impact these videos will have on your bottom line, and I would hate for you to have to wait to move forward with these videos. We could either do a 10% deposit or a 20% deposit instead of the 50% deposit to reduce the impact on your budget for this quarter. Would you prefer 10% or 20%?"

If there is no room for you to adjust to overcome the client's concerns, focus on the benefits of the videos to the client. You can say something along the lines of, "It's completely understandable that this project was not originally included in the budget. It sounds like this project would have an immediate effect on your team's budget. With that being said, over the next few months, these videos have the possibility to provide a significant boost to your sales through _____ and _____ . By looking at _____, we see that it's likely your team will experience a net benefit of ___ with the use of this video. Let's take a look at this against the other areas that are currently being budgeted for. How does that sound?"

These same principles can be applied to any type of objections the client might provide. They don't like the length of the video you are proposing? They don't like the proposed shots? They want to do a voiceover instead of an interview? Ask the questions to identify the objection so that you can make adjustments and overcome the obstacles.

Once you have overcome all objections and the client is ready to close, send the invoice for the deposit, and lock in the next item on the calendar whether that be a shoot date, a preproduction planning meeting, or any other item that you need to meet for. If you are using a contract, send that over as well. Once all of your materials are completed, you've locked in the sale.

The third phase of the 3-Phase Approach to 6-Figure Sales is the key to increasing your long-term earning potential. We'll talk about this phase in the next chapter.

Chapter 18

REPEAT BUSINESS

R epeat business is exactly what it sounds like. It is when you do business with a client that you have already done business with before. Getting repeat clients is the key to scaling your business and building long-term success. According to a study by Invesp, similar to findings cited earlier in the book, it costs five times the amount to acquire a new customer as it takes to keep an existing one,[15] so not only does it cost less, it can earn you significantly more. Another significant reason I mention this study is that it goes on to say that existing customers are 50% more likely to try new products and spend 31% more than new customers are. This means it is cheaper and more lucrative for you to earn repeat business.

Lastly, it is the easiest way to scale your business. If a client only turns into one sale, that means to make more money, you have to find a new client. You will find yourself in a constant race to find new clients. If a client turns out to be a lifelong client that turns into multiple sales, each new client creates a compounding effect on the sales of your business. You will see your sales follow an exponential curve. Each sale turns into more sales, which turns into more sales, which turns into more sales.

So, what is the key to earning repeat business? There are two stages to securing repeat business: BC (Before Completion) and AD (After Delivery). First, let's take a look at the BC stage.

Two Stages of Earning Repeat Business

BC (Before Completion)

The BC (Before Completion) stage refers to everything from the point of the sale until the completion of the project. Average videographers slack off once the sale is made. They've cashed the client's check, and now they can move on to the next sale. They will complete the project, but they're unconcerned about creating the best video(s) they can and they no longer prioritize the client. This is the attitude that turns clients into one-time customers. The first key to turning clients into lifelong customers is over-delivering.

Over-Deliver

Over-delivering means going above and beyond for the client and delivering on more than you promised. Have you ever heard someone say, "Joe always over-promises and under-delivers." The failing videographer over-promises and under-delivers. The six-figure videographer under-promises and over-delivers.

What does this look like in practice? This starts with the sales process. Don't write checks you can't cash. Don't promise items to the client that you can't deliver on. Be realistic with expectations while framing your product in the best light possible.

Follow Through

Follow through on promises you make. It's easy to fall into a bad habit of telling a client you will provide them certain items by certain dates and not follow through on those promises. When you tell a client you are going to provide them something by a certain time, be accountable, and get back to them with the items by the time you promised.

If obstacles arise, and you aren't able to meet the promised deadline any longer, be honest and quick to provide an update. Let's say you promised to provide the finished video to a client by Tuesday, and Monday has arrived and you know you will not be finished with the project by the next day. Be honest with the client, be proactive in providing an update, and provide them a new timeline for completion. You can say something like:

Hey, Jennifer, I had originally told you that I would have the video complete by Tuesday, but I wanted to provide you with an update. On Friday I was working on a segment of the video that ended up taking a bit longer than

I had originally planned. With this being said, it is going to take me one more day to finish the video. I sincerely apologize for the delay, and I look forward to sending you the video by Wednesday at 5 p.m.

If you are upfront with the client, proactive in providing an update, and let them know a new timeline for completion, most clients will be understanding. With that being said, don't make a habit of missing deadlines. When you provide a client with a timeline, follow through.

Be Present

Have you ever been looking into a product or service, then the second that you signed the dotted line, the sales representative was nowhere to be found to assist with any challenges? Were you frustrated? Did you feel taken advantage of?

This is an easy way to burn a bridge and turn potential lifelong clients into one-time clients. Be available, and be happy to answer questions the client may have as you work through the project. When they send you a message, get back to them quickly. Don't get lazy. When you look at an email, don't say to yourself, "I'll get back to that later." Respond to it right away. With the technology we have nowadays, it's easy to be an effective communicator.

I promise your clients will notice this, and it will earn you a lot of money in the long run. You will see clients come back to you time and time again because you were easy to work with and easy to get a hold of.

Now that we've reviewed three keys to earning repeat business in the BC stage of the project, it's time to talk about the AD stage. Let's talk about items to focus on after project delivery.

AD (After Delivery)

Show Appreciation

After delivering the final video to the client, average videographers make the costly mistake of sending them a half-hearted thank you message via email. Six-figure videographers go the extra mile to show a more sincere appreciation to clients in the form of a hand-written thank-you letter. After you have finished the project and sent the final video to the client, write them a hand-written thank-you note showing appreciation that they selected you for their videography needs, and outline how much you enjoyed the project.

Hand-written thank-you letters are a powerful tool that fewer and fewer people utilize in today's technological world. This makes them all the more powerful. A small token of appreciation in the form of a thank-you letter will earn you impressive sums of repeat business. Structure your thank-you letter as follows:

- Greeting
- Thank you
- Express enjoyment working on the project
- Close

Here is an example:

Dear John and Team,

Thank you for trusting me to create your corporate video for Excellent Lawn Care and Services. I sincerely enjoyed the time I spent working with your team on this project. I hope that this video continues earning you new business for many years to come. Please let me know if you are ever in need of future video assistance. You can find my email and cell phone on the business cards I have provided for your convenience. Take care!

This small act of appreciation is going to go a long way in building deeper relationships with your clients and earning you future business. If you want to take further advantage of the power of thank-you letters, send one to every client after you meet with them for a presentation. Whether you close, don't close, or haven't heard back, send one. If you closed, this will build further trust heading into the project. If you don't close, this might push them to reconsider. And if you haven't heard back, this might be what seals the deal for you.

Provide Continued Value

Average videographers forget about past clients once they have finished a project. Six-figure videographers provide continued value to their clients at every opportunity available. What does it mean to provide continued value?

Anytime you see something that a client could find valuable, send it to them. Blog posts, YouTube videos, articles, newsletters, books—anything that you know the client will find value in, pass it along to them. This accomplishes three things:

1. Builds trust
2. Deepens relationships
3. Keeps you on their mind

When you send a value-packed article to a client, the client is going to think, "Wow! They remembered that I mentioned ____ during a casual conversation we had. They really listen to me." As you build trust, the relationship with your clients deepens. It's nearly impossible to build trust without deepening a relationship. Deeper relationships mean more projects.

Lastly, this action keeps you on their mind. Clients can't do business with you if they're not thinking about you. Inversely, if you're regularly on a client's mind, they are going to find ways to do business with you. Being on their mind will keep them thinking about ways they can utilize you to grow their business.

Share Other Services

The final way to earn repeat business is to share other services with your clients. It is likely that your clients could benefit from a number of videos that you could create for them. After a client hires you for one project, they are likely to hire you for a future project. In order to make this happen, you need to make them aware of other services or videos that you can produce for them.

After you finish a project, follow the steps above, and after an appropriate amount of time, suggest a new video project that they could benefit from. Don't bombard them looking for new business the moment you finish a project. This can come off as salesly. Instead, after an appropriate amount of time, share other videos with them that you think they could benefit from.

Another great way to share other services is if you have a big win with a client in a similar industry. Let's say that you created a website video for a client. After you finished the project, another client in a similar industry hired you to create social media videos for them. The client shares with you that the social media videos brought in a big boost in sales for them. Share this with the other client if you think they could benefit from these types of videos.

Say something similar to:

> Hi, Joe. I hope you've been well since we finished our last project. Over the past month, I produced a series of social media videos for Scott Scottsdale, the owner of Picture Perfect Picnic Tables. Scott experienced a 50% boost in sales after posting his videos to social media for the last month. I think that you could experience a similar boost

in sales for Rock Solid Rocking Chairs with the same type of video content for your social media channels.

I'm available tomorrow at 11 a.m. and Wednesday at 3 p.m. to chat more about how we could produce similar videos for Rock Solid Rocking Chairs. What time works best for you to jump on a call?

With these six strategies, you are going to unlock unlimited earning potential for yourself and your business. Repeat business is the key to making more money with less work on the front-end. Once you start locking in repeat business, sit back and watch as your business grows at an exponential rate.

You have the sales strategies you need to turn your videography business into a six-figure videography business. Now is where the rubber meets the road. In his book *The Law of Success in Sixteen Lessons*, Napoleon Hill writes, "Power grows out of organized knowledge, but mind you, it grows out of it, through application and use."[16] Without application and use, knowledge is nothing.

How do we apply knowledge? Through action. What spurs us to take action? Setting goals. It's time to set hard goals that will help make your dreams a reality. In the next chapter, we'll talk about how to set your goals.

Chapter 19
SET YOUR BUSINESS GOALS

Don't Be a Starving Artist

I was sitting on the couch watching TV with my family. It was a Saturday morning in the fall, six months after I had thrown in the towel on working full-time as owner of my own videography business. I was working a corporate job and attempting to cherish every last minute of my weekend before Monday rolled around, and I had to swallow the bitter reality of waking up to punch the clock to work a job that left me unfulfilled. Fall Saturdays for my family typically are spent tuning in to college football. On this particular Saturday the family was all together at my brother's house.

While I had given up my ambitions of working full-time as a videographer, my passion for video remained. I still spent endless hours on YouTube studying the art of video production. I binged tutorials on lighting setups, I analyzed videos breaking down audio capture, and I kept in touch with every new product that hit the market. At that point, I felt I could walk onto a Hollywood set and skate by in 80% of the jobs being completed.

As the football game cut to commercial break, a commercial for a local car dealership came onto the screen. I tore the commercial to shreds. "The lighting on that guy is way too harsh! You can see the green screen bleeding through on the outline of that lady! These animations are terrible!"

I thought, "I have all of the knowledge the people making these commercials have. Why didn't I get these opportunities?" I was jealous.

You know what doesn't pay the bills? Jealousy.

You can have all of the videography knowledge in the world, but without application, you'll be a starving artist.

This chapter is about setting goals using the sales strategies we reviewed earlier in this section to take your videography business from floundering to flourishing. Action is where the money is.

The SMART Goal Framework

It's time for you to outline your sales goals. When setting goals, ensure that they adhere to the **SMART** goals framework. SMART is an acronym that stands for: specific, measurable, achievable, relevant, and time-bound. Let's further break that down.

Specific: Specific goals are goals that outline a clear action. Goals that are abstract aren't helpful. For example, a goal that lacks specificity would be, "I will contact five business owners a week." A specific goal would be, "Each week, I am going to find email addresses for five owners of five CrossFit gyms and email them offering a free 'workout demo' video to build trust and offer a brand video on the backend."

Measurable: You need goals that you can actively track progress toward. Goals that can't be tracked are bad goals. For example, a goal that can't be tracked would be, "I will grow my business over the next quarter." There is not measurable growth in this goal and in what way would you like to grow your business? Increase revenue? Increase profit? Grow the number of clients you booked from last month? A measurable goal would be, "This quarter, I want to grow my business's profit by 10% in comparison to the previous quarter. I will do this by …" Now you have a measurable goal that you can work toward.

Achievable: You need goals that are realistically achievable. This doesn't mean you shouldn't dream big. Set lofty goals for yourself as well. Who knows? When you run your own business, the sky's the limit. You could have a deal fall in your lap that you never would have dreamed of landing.

Setting achievable goals doesn't mean you can't exceed those goals. It just makes it more likely that you will move in the right direction. Have you ever had a friend who told you they were going to accomplish a ridiculous goal like, "I'm going to lose 20 pounds in two weeks." As soon as they said it, you knew there was no chance they were going to achieve their goal. Then a few days later, they'd completely given up on the goal?

That's the pitfall of setting goals that are unachievable. Set a goal for yourself that you would be excited to achieve, but you also know is realistically possible. An example of an unattainable goal for most people just getting started would be, "I will make $10 million profit in my first six months in business." Unless you're signing your rookie contract to play starting point-guard for the nearest NBA team, this is probably not an achievable goal.

A better goal would be, "I will email 20 marketing directors for insurance agencies each week providing social media videos I have created for an insurance agent with the goal of booking them for a discovery call."

Relevant: It's important that your goal be relevant to the success of your business. Sometimes we can get so caught up in the inner workings of our business that we forget the ultimate goal is to make money doing something we love. Don't get lost in the weeds and set goals that don't lead to your business's success.

For example, let's say that your business specializes in producing safety training videos for manufacturing companies. You gain all of your clients by presenting at industry trade shows. Your target client is typically not on social media. An example of an irrelevant goal would be, "I will post to my company's Instagram page five days per week for the entire quarter." This goal does not bring you closer to your end goal of driving revenue for your business.

Does it make you feel good posting to your Instagram? Sure. Do you get more customers from posting to Instagram?

No. A better goal would be, "I will attend two trade shows per week for the entire quarter and pass out at least five business cards at each trade show." This goal is relevant to the success of your business.

Time-Bound: It's important that your goals have some sort of timeline associated with them. It's easy to fall into the trap of setting goals without setting a timeline. Goals without a timeline are goals that are never accomplished. This is particularly important for those that fall into the category of being procrastinators. (Don't worry; you're not alone. So am I.)

Oftentimes, we procrastinators are capable of producing exceptional work; however, this work will all be completed at the eleventh hour right before our deadline. An example of a goal that is not time-bound would be, "I will call five optometry practices." There's no deadline for this goal. A better goal would be, "This quarter, I will call five optometry practices each week by 5 p.m. on Friday offering a free social media video with the goal of converting the practice into a paid client for four social media videos per month."

Now that you have the framework for your goals, it's time to create your outbound sales goals, your inbound sales goals, and your goals for earning repeat business. When it comes to allocating time toward outbound sales versus inbound sales, I want you to use the 80/20 rule. Apply 80% of your time toward outbound sales and 20% of your time toward inbound sales. Outbound sales should be the driving force behind new business, particularly when you're first working toward that six-figure mark.

Think of sales like a big cake. Outbound sales compose the sponge. This is what makes up 80% to 90% of the cake. Inbound sales is the icing on the cake. Tastes delicious, but only makes up 10% to 20% of the cake. If you try to make the entire cake out of it, you're going to fall flat. Over time, you will see that your inbound sales goals and your goals pertaining to repeat business will start to grow while the need to rely on outbound sales diminishes. For now, let's start by setting your outbound sales goals.

Outbound Sales Goals

When it comes to setting goals, the focus should be around the controllables. Another great way to think about this is setting activity goals, not production goals. You can control your activity, but you can't always control the production. Setting goals around production can ultimately lead to frustration and burnout.

For example, let's say that you set a production goal of earning $10,000 this month in sales. This goal is focused on the outcome, not the activity. If you do all of the work you estimate you need to in order to hit your goal, but you end the month at $7,000 in sales, you would be frustrated because you missed your goal. In all reality, you don't have full control over the percentage of sales you land. Some months will be higher, and some months will be lower.

Not hitting your goal might create discouragement and lead to you not working as hard the next month. In all reality, it's possible you could do the same work the next month and end the month at $13,000. This is why it is important to set goals for yourself based on activity. What does this look like? The main activity you can control in outbound sales is prospecting. Why is this? You can't control how many people answer your calls or return your emails, but you c control how many calls you make or emails you send.

For this reason, when setting outbound sales goals, focus on setting prospecting goals. Set a benchmark for yourself of how many prospecting actions you want to accomplish throughout the month. To do this, first set a yearly income goal for yourself. Don't measure your success based on this goal, but this will help you estimate how many prospecting actions you need to take for the month. Fill in the blank below:

I want to earn a total of $_____ this year.

For the purposes of this example, let's say that number is $100,000. Next, take that number and break it into a monthly goal. To earn $100,000, you would need to average $8,300 per month. We then want to further break that number down into a weekly goal. This would average out to roughly $2,000 per week.

Now you know what you want to earn each week. From here, look at the average cost of the videos you create. Let's say you specialize in brand videos for commercial builders. Your typical brand video is $6,000. This means you should be averaging one project every three weeks to meet your goal of $100,000 for the year. Now work backwards from here to figure out what your prospecting goals should be.

When you're starting off, you won't know on average how many prospecting actions it takes for you to book a discovery call and how many discovery calls on average you convert into presentations and how many presentations on average you convert into sales. With enough time, you will figure out these numbers. At the beginning, use your best guess. You will quickly learn whether that number is too low or too high.

For this example, let's say it takes you 10 cold emails to book a discovery call. It then takes you three discovery calls to book a presentation. Then one out of every three presentations turns into a paid client. This means, on average, you will need to send around 90 cold emails to land a project. Ninety cold emails over a three-week period, working five days per week comes out to six cold emails a day.

You now have your daily prospecting goal. Send out six cold emails a day. As you strive to hit this goal each day, you will gain a better understanding of your true averages. Maybe it only takes five cold emails to book a discovery call, maybe it takes 12. Adjust your activity goals as you gain a better understanding of your averages.

Achieving your prospecting goals will be what creates a strong foundation of sales for your business. Now, let's review the icing on the cake, inbound sales.

Inbound Sales Goals

While prospecting to achieve your outbound sales goals will be what drives the most business, particularly at the onset, we don't want to neglect the activities that will lead to long-term inbound sales. Inbound sales goals are harder to create as we have less control over the number of leads that come in through marketing efforts. With that being said, this is still an important part of the business that we should be putting time and effort into.

Just with our outbound sales goals, we should place the focus on the activity that we can control for inbound sales. This comes down to creating the marketing materials that provide opportunities for prospects to locate our business and reach out to inquire about our services. For example, if you know that your target client spends a lot of time on social media, you could set a goal of creating a certain number of social media posts per week.

Additionally, if you find that a lot of your target clients use Google to find a videographer in your niche, you could set a certain amount of time each week writing blog posts for your website to improve your SEO. Maybe you discover that your target client spends a lot of time utilizing email. You could spend time each week working on building a weekly newsletter to send out to your target audience.

Identify where your target client spends most of their time, and structure your marketing strategy accordingly. Inbound sales are a great way to earn business and supplement the sales you make through outbound sales.

Lastly, we have repeat business goals.

Repeat Business Goals

Depending on your niche, repeat business could be the biggest opportunity for scaling your business to, and beyond, the $100,000 mark. As I mentioned previously, repeat clients are 50% more likely to try new products and spend 31% more than new customers are. This means time saved and higher sales, ultimately leading to greater earning potential.

You should be spending the necessary amount of time tending to your past clients to earn repeat business. The ultimate goal is to build up your client base to the point where you don't need to prospect because you have more work than you can handle from repeat clients, or you can build a team to allow you to take on more clients and earn even more money.

When it comes to setting goals for repeat clients, you should ultimately be planning outreach to all of your previous clients that you would like to do business with again. Start by creating a list of your clients. This does not have to be anything fancy. You can simply keep a spreadsheet listing all of the clients' names, emails, phone numbers, and a column for the date you reached out to them last. If you have a past client that you would prefer to not take on again because they were a "C client," then add them to the list but note that they were a C.

We have a free Google Spreadsheet template that you can use to create your list. To download it, go to Chapter 19 of the Film to Freedom companion course (you can access the companion course for free at www.videography-university. com/course). Once you have your spreadsheet, you should reach out to each of these clients once a quarter. You might be getting sweaty palms, thinking, "I don't want to reach out to my past clients and sound salesy." Remember, our definition of sales is centered on creating a partnership. Our goal with reaching out to past clients is to provide value, not to *pester*. What are ways that you can reach out to past clients to provide value?

One of my favorite ways to connect with past clients is to send them a gift card. Would you be upset if someone sent you a $5 gift card via email? I sure know I wouldn't! Utilize your preferred method of communication. You can write them a letter and send them a gift card inside of it, or you can email them and send a virtual gift card. My favorite way to do this is to send an email with the subject line, "Coffee's on me today!" Then inside I will send a virtual gift card to Starbucks or another coffee shop.

I will add in a note, thanking them for being a past client and letting them know if they need any videography services that I'm available. This is a great way to connect with past clients by leading with value. Are you thinking, "Five dollars for a client each quarter is expensive." I challenge you to utilize this method for two quarters. After testing it out, I feel confident that you will be amazed at the ROI.

Let's say that you have 20 clients that you would love to work with again. Sending a $5 gift card to 20 clients will cost you $100 a quarter and $200 over the span of two quarters. Let's say the average project for these clients was $3,000. I bet you will book at least one, if not more, clients on additional projects through this method. That doesn't even include the referrals that could come out of this surprising act of kindness. That is $200 spent for $3,000 in sales. A 15-time return on investment. Companies would *kill* for that kind of ROI. Give this method a shot, and watch the sales roll in.

Another great way to stay top of mind with clients is engaging with them on social media. Social media provides an avenue to foster continuous communication and touch points with previous clients. A survey by Social Media Examiner discovered that 96% of small businesses utilize social media marketing.[17] 76% of small businesses use social media for their business. According to Business DIT, 93.79% of all businesses utilize social media.[18] What does this mean for you? No matter who your target client is, it's likely they are on social media, and this is a great opportunity for you to stay on their mind.

Most businesses are not receiving a substantial amount of engagement on their social media channels. Let's face it, a lot of business owners don't know how to leverage this tool to create a lot of engagement. (Time for you to offer some additional services. ;)) For this reason, engaging with past clients on social media is likely to be noticed and well received.

Put yourself in the shoes of the business owner. Let's play out a hypothetical scenario. Let's say we have a lawyer named Jerry. Jerry owns his own law firm. Jerry knows that social media is a powerful tool and that he should be on it, so Jerry decides it's time to take action. Jerry has an Instagram account that his daughter created for him five years ago that has two pictures of his dog, one motivational quote, and a picture slideshow of his most recent vacation he went on with his wife. Jerry starts posting infographics about law on his Instagram. He does this consistently for six months.

Crickets.

Then, on his latest post he receives a comment that says, "Great info, Jerry! Thanks for sharing," from the videographer he hired to shoot a website video for him a few weeks back. Immediate mood boost! Remember, people do business with people they know, like, and trust. You just put yourself top of mind for Jerry, effectively accomplishing the "know" part of the equation. You just created a positive interaction building further "likeability." And Jerry already did business with you once, so the odds are he already "trusts" you. Jerry is going to start thinking of new ways that he can utilize your services. Maybe some engaging video content for his Instagram account?

Another added benefit is that your comment is visible to all of Jerry's followers. Maybe another lawyer who could use your services follows Jerry. Do you ever see a comment on social media that sparks your curiosity, so you take a look at the profile for the account? If Jerry's lawyer friend looks at your profile, they will hopefully see all of the amazing work that you have done for past clients. You might have just earned yourself a new client. See how powerful it can be to engage with past clients on social media?

It's important that you don't go overboard with this strategy and become overbearing. If you're commenting on every post a client puts up or engaging too much with the client on social media, it might come off as salesy. Be genuine, don't be overbearing, and social media engagement can be a great way to earn repeat business. Block time off in your calendar to engage with past clients on social media. Utilize your list to ensure that you are interacting with each client.

Be strategic about the way you approach this method. Many people, myself included, are guilty of being passive users of social media. Between meetings we'll take a look at Facebook, or we'll hop on Instagram while we're exporting a video. Don't fall into this trap. Passive use of social media equates to wasted time. Plan out how you will utilize these platforms, and schedule out time when you will do so.

Lastly, you can reach out to make past clients aware of other videos you offer. A great way to do this is to share work you did for a different client in a similar industry. Let's say that you created a conference highlight video for an industry organization. The video consisted of B-roll from the conference with music in the background. The client was thrilled with the video. A few weeks later, another company hires you to shoot customer testimonials for them. You complete the project, send the finished videos to the client, and they love the final videos.

Almost every business can benefit from testimonials. At that point, you could send the testimonial videos you created to the first client and say,

> *Hey, Christine! I hope you've been well since the conference in July. I was thinking about you and the team the other day. A few days back I captured testimonial content for another client in a similar industry. As I was capturing the content, I thought to myself, "Testimonials would be a great way for Christine and her team to boost attendance at next year's conference." Below are links to the testimonials I captured for my other client. Take a look, and let me know if your team would be interested in this type of video content to increase attendance at next year's event.*

You're demonstrating to the client that you're actively thinking about them, and you're providing value by showing them a marketing tool that they could use to help grow their organization. You can perform this outreach as opportunities present themselves, but a more effective way is to structure this type of outreach. The truth is, many types of videos would benefit a large number of your clients.

Most clients can utilize testimonials. Most clients can utilize a brand video. Most clients can utilize some sort of product/service tutorial video. Most clients can utilize social media videos. Utilize your repeat client spreadsheet and schedule time each quarter to reach out to past clients to share your recent work with them. The key is to detail how the videos can be a benefit to them. The heart of the message should always be about them. You're sharing this work with them because it could benefit their business.

These are just a few of the countless ways you can stay in contact with past clients. No matter the method that works best for you, the key is to plan how you will do it, schedule when you will do it, and then do it. As Winston Churchill once said, "He who fails to plan is planning to fail." Create your plan, and take action on it. Share your plan with your accountability partner, so they can keep you accountable to following through. Once you follow through, you will be amazed at how much more you can earn through repeat business.

Now that we've talked about setting business goals, let's talk about setting personal goals to help you make the jump to going full-time with your videography business. If you don't have any ambitions of going full-time with your business, feel free to jump to Chapter 21.

Action Time:

Outbound Sales Goals

1. Select a target income goal for your business for the year. Select a goal that feels ambitious, but attainable.

2. Use the current knowledge you have along with your best judgment to reverse engineer how many outreaches it will take you to land a discovery meeting in your niche, how many discovery meetings it will take to book a presentation, and how many presentations it will take to book a project.

3. Use those values to identify how many prospecting actions you should take a day to achieve your yearly sales goal.

4. Write these numbers down and track them daily.

Inbound Sales Goals

5. Identify what platforms your clients are spending most of their time on and where they are most likely to find your business.

6. Create weekly action goals to create content to foster inbound sales through these platforms, e.g., create three Instagram posts per week, create one blog post on your website per week, create one podcast episode per week.

Repeat Business Goals

7. List out all of your current and past clients who you would like to do business with again. Make a copy of the free Client Spreadsheet in Chapter 19 of the Film to

Freedom companion course (you can access the companion course for free at www.videography-university.com/course).

8. Identify the method of outreach you will perform for your clients each quarter. You should be reaching out to each client at least once a quarter.

9. Create weekly goals for reaching out to the necessary number of clients each week.

10. Track your progress on your outreach performance. If you want help staying accountable with performing the outreach and tracking your progress or with achieving your outbound or inbound sales goals, book a call with us at www.videography-university.com/apply.

Section 6

Next Steps

Chapter 20

SET YOUR PERSONAL GOALS

If you fail to plan, you plan to fail. In the fall of my senior year of college, my friend Ryan Willis made a challenge with me. He challenged me to run a marathon with him the following fall. Being a fitness enthusiast and not one to turn down a challenge, I told him he was on. Ryan spent the next few months researching and organizing a training plan for us. We had no ambitions of casually completing the marathon. We had a goal of completing the marathon in under 3 hours and 30 minutes, putting us at an average pace at or below 7 minutes and 59 seconds per mile.

Spring rolled around, and Ryan shared the training plan with me. We had roughly six months to prepare. Our training consisted of three "short" runs during the week and one "long" run on the weekend. "I got this!" I told myself as I looked at the schedule. The first week I accomplished all of my runs. By the end of the week, although the race was still quite some time in the future, I could already see the finish line. Week two came, and I missed my second run of the week. I was busy on Wednesday, and my run fell to the back of my to-do list never to be accomplished.

I wasn't worried, I was notching my runs at a sub-seven-minute per mile pace so far. I could miss one run. Right? As the weeks rolled on, missing one run turned into missing two runs, turned into missing three runs, and after a few months, I was only accomplishing my "long" run with Ryan on the weekend. It was a Sunday morning three months out from the marathon. Ryan and I had just run 15 miles the day before. My only run for the week. I stood up to get out of bed, and a shooting pain ran up my leg. Oh, no.

I tried to walk it off throughout the day, but the pain persisted. By midweek the pain subsided, and I attempted a run. I woke up the next morning feeling okay. There was a hint of the pain, but it wasn't as bad as it had been a few days prior. The weekend came, and it was time for our long run. I was too stubborn to give up. I ran 16 miles with Ryan. I spent the next two days limping.

After a serious heart to heart with my then girlfriend, now wife, I came to an agreement that it was not a smart decision to continue on with running the marathon in two months. My body was not in proper condition to handle the toll the miles were taking on it, and it was nobody else's fault but mine. We settled on a compromise. I'd take a few days off, and if I was able to resume limited training with no pain, I would run the half marathon instead. Two months later,

I crossed the finish line after completing the half marathon instead of the marathon I had set out to run.

How did this happen? I failed to plan. I had an outline of what I needed to do, but I did not plan out how I was going to make it a reality. I did not plan when I was going to run each day. Because of this, on busy days, I didn't end up running. I didn't plan how I was going to properly stretch and prepare my body for the miles I would be running. Because of this, injuries happened. And finally, I didn't prepare a way to keep myself accountable. If I had created accountability check-ins with Ryan, I would have been more likely to stick to the training.

If you fail to plan, you plan to fail.

Side Hustle vs. Full-Time

There are two directions that you can go with your videography business. You can either use your business as a side hustle, or you can plan to go full-time with it. The first thing you need to ask yourself is, "What are my goals for my future?" Here are a few questions to consider:

1. Do you enjoy working for somebody else, or do you want the freedom of being your own boss?
2. Do you need the consistency of a paycheck from an employer, or do you like the ability to have unlimited earning potential?

3. Do you find personal fulfillment in working for another company, or do you feel more fulfilled in building a business of your own?

There's no right or wrong answer to these questions. This is simply a question of what's right for you. I have a friend who is a wedding videographer. He is a full-time teacher as well. He has two kids, and the consistency of his teaching job works for him. He has no plans of leaving his job any time soon. He uses his free time during the summer to shoot weddings. He is making $30,000-plus each year in the summer months with his wedding videography side hustle. This is what works for him.

For me, I could never shake the dream of being my own boss, having ultimate control over my life, and having unlimited earning potential. Pursuing videography as a full-time business was the right option for me. At the end of the day, you need to determine what the right path is for you.

Evaluate your goals and your circumstances, and then make a decision. There is nothing wrong with starting off with videography as a side hustle and then deciding later down the line to transition to running your videography business as your full-time job. I worked a 9-to-5 for two years while I grew my videography business on the side.

If you decide to pursue the route of running your videography business part-time, you can skip to the next chapter in this section, as the remainder of this chapter is focused toward those with a goal of earning enough to transition to working full-time as owner and operator of their videography business. For those looking to earn enough to go full-time, it's time to set some hard goals for yourself.

When I made the decision to pursue videography full-time, I set goals for myself that I had to achieve before I would make the jump to leaving my 9-to-5. I was 24 at the time, but I was already married when I set my goal of running my own business full-time. While my wife and I did not yet have kids, I still owed it to her to be able to provide financial security for our family. We had financial responsibilities in the way of housing, insurance, living expenses, and savings goals. It would have been unfair for me to put all of that aside for my own dreams.

With these responsibilities, it was important to me that I made this transition with as much forethought and preparation as possible. I laid out two goals that I had to achieve before I would allow myself to make the jump:

1. I had to save up $50,000 worth of money from video projects. This was roughly equivalent to my yearly salary from my 9-to-5.
2. I had to be making at least 75% of my salary from video projects for a rolling six-month period. This meant I needed to be earning at least $18,750 for a rolling six-month period of time.

My savings goal was a safety net. By saving $50,000, I knew that I could pay my salary into our savings account for a year if no projects were to come. My earnings goal was to prove to myself I could make continuous income from projects for an extended period of time. I figured if I could earn 75% of my salary for six months straight while working 40-plus hours a week at my full-time job, then I should be able to earn at least 25% more when I would be committing my entire week to my videography business.

By the time I put in my two weeks at my 9-to-5, I had saved up $53,363.72 and had made $37,373.37 in the previous six months, twice my goal of $18,750. I was quickly learning the earning potential when running a videography business. These two points of security were big stress-relievers when I put in my two weeks. I knew that I could hit a significant dry spell in projects, and I would still be able to put money into our bank account.

The following six months, I discovered the real potential of being able to commit all of my time to my videography business. At my corporate job, I was making roughly $4,583 a month. In the six months after I went full-time with my videography business, I made $84,825.78. An average of $14,137.63 per month. I was making over three times my salary.

I share these numbers with you to show what is possible when running your own videography business full-time. When I was in my phase of doubt, I didn't know if videography was a viable route to earning a good living. There was no income breakdown on Google for running your own videography business. I heard project rates here and there, but

I was never able to find hard numbers on what people in the industry were making on an annual basis.

Now let me be clear, by no means is it a guarantee that you will make the same amount right away. It's possible, but I had built up a solid client base by the time I went full-time with my business. With that being said, through continuous hard work, you can make more money than most will ever be able to. In addition, your potential is uncapped. The sky's the limit.

If you find yourself in the bucket of someone who wants to pursue this as a full-time career, I recommend doing the following:

1. Identify how much money you want to have saved as a safety net before you leave your 9-to-5.
2. Identify how much money you want to be earning for a rolling six-month period of time before you leave your 9-to-5.

These numbers are going to be personal to you, your family, and your unique situation. Maybe they're similar to mine, maybe they're more than mine, maybe they're less than mine. Whatever the case may be, figure out what these numbers are, and start working toward them. My mission was to save at least 12 months' worth of my salary for my first goal and earn at least 75% of my salary over a six-month period for my second goal.

Figure out your goals, and write them down. I also recommend going to Chapter 20 of the Film to Freedom companion course where we've provided a PDF document you can use to write your goals on (to access the companion course for free go to (www.videography-university.com/course).

This brings me to my last piece of advice when it comes to saving to make the leap to full-time. My advice is simple, but hard: save, save, save! As videographers, most of us are eager to purchase the newest shiniest piece of gear that just hit the market. We want to buy new cameras, new lenses, new lights, and the list goes on. When you are preparing to make the jump to full-time, save as much as you possibly can. Ignore the urge to purchase the next latest piece of gear. I promise 90% of improving your craft is about acquiring knowledge and experience as opposed to spending money on new gear.

At this stage, the only time you should spend money on new gear is if you will lose money if you don't purchase something. If you are unable to capture a project because you don't have a piece of gear and that means you will lose more money than it would cost you to purchase the gear, then at that point you should purchase the piece of equipment. Outside of that, save up every last dollar you can.

Your biggest asset when you make the leap to going full-time with your videography business is going to be your savings. By having a security blanket in the form of your savings, you accomplish three things:

1. You won't need to accept jobs out of desperation.
2. You buy yourself peace of mind.
3. You open yourself up to long-term opportunities.

You won't need to accept jobs out of desperation.

When I was starting in videography, I had the mentality that I needed to accept every job that came my way. I felt bad turning clients away. If a prospective client came to me saying they wanted a video, but they only had a budget of $500, I tried to find a way to force my services into their budget. This ultimately led to frustration on both sides of the equation. I was frustrated because I wasn't being compensated for what I thought I was worth, and the client was frustrated when they expected future projects for the same rates, but I quoted more.

When you have a buffer in savings, you aren't desperate for cash, so you don't have to service clients that are outside of your niche. You can refer these clients out to other, more suitable videographers, which ultimately is a better use of your time. This leaves you happy because you can focus on projects better suited toward you, this leaves the client happy because they are getting the services they need, and it builds a great referral partner in the other videographer who will refer clients to you in the future.

You buy yourself peace of mind.

When we are stressed, we don't think clearly. If you're worrying about how you're going to pay the bills, provide for your family, or invest in your future, your stress is going to get in the way of you being the best business owner you can be. Having that chunk of change in your savings account is going to keep your stress level low and allow you to show up as the best business owner you can be each day.

You're going to open yourself up to long-term opportunities.

Think of the breakdown of your client base as a split between A, B, and C clients. A clients are your dream clients. These are the clients you one day hope to build your entire business around. These clients don't come around every day, but when they do, you are doing the projects you love, and you're eating well for the next month.

B clients are your day-to-day clients. These are the clients you are servicing most often. They might not be the ideal projects you want to work on, but they pay well, and they always show up.

C clients are the time-drainers. C clients are outside of your ideal scope of projects, don't pay the best, and tend to take advantage of your time. These are the clients that provide you a tinge of anxiety when you see an inquiry come through. You take these clients on when business is looking sparse from your A and B clients.

When you have a safety net in the bank, you give yourself the opportunity to work with more A clients because your calendar isn't booked up with projects for C clients. You don't have to turn down business from an A client because you've already committed your next few weeks to a C. You know the bills will be handled, and you can make it on your Bs until your next A comes along.

I've wasted a lot of time on C clients in the past. Don't fall into that trap.

Action Time:

1. Figure out the savings and earnings goals you want to achieve before you make the leap to going full-time with your videography business. Once again, these guidelines are going to be unique to you and your situation. You need to figure out what the numbers are based on all the factors in your life.

2. To help identify your goals, try to fill in the blank in the two statements below:

    I want to have $_____ saved as a security fund before I make the jump to going full-time.

    I want to have earned $_____ over a rolling six-month period before I make the jump to going full-time.

3. Lay out any additional guidelines that you may need for yourself as well. Then start saving. This is the action that will make your dream a reality.

4. I recommend going to Chapter 20 of the Film to Freedom companion course where we have created a PDF that you can print off and use to set your savings/earnings goals. To access the course for free, go to <u>www.videography-university.com/course</u>.

Chapter 21

YOUR IMPLEMENTATION PLAN

Realize Your "Why"

My hope is that this book has motivated you to take the action that will turn your videography business into a six-figure income. Look back on your "why" from Section 2. What is driving you to make this dream a reality? Do you have ambitions of escaping the life of a 9-to-5? Do you have dreams of financial freedom? Do you hope to realize the personal satisfaction of running your own business full-time? Videography is a skill that has the power to make these dreams a reality. It's all about taking the action necessary to bring these goals to life.

In this book, you learned the keys to building a strong foundation for your business. You discovered the power of specializing in a niche and how to identify your niche. You learned the four keys to creating a formidable brand. And finally, you studied the 3-Phase Approach to 6-Figure Sales.

Now it's time to take action. It's time to get started on your journey to turning your videography business into a six-figure Income. The most important step is to get started.

We Have the Tools

When my wife and I bought our first house, we were excited to move in and make the place our own. When we stepped foot through the front door for the first time, we looked around and realized it was due time for the inside of the house to get a fresh coat of paint. We had a handyman in the first week to take a look at a few electrical outlets throughout the house. I told him that I was going to start painting the house the following day.

"Oh, yea!" he said. "I do painting as well if you're interested in having some help." He handed me his business card. "I usually charge around $250 per room."

"How much would it cost to have you paint this entire first floor?" I asked him.

He looked around surveying the room. The first floor had a family room, a kitchen, a dining room, and a small sunroom. It was the largest space in the house and consequently was most in need of painting.

"The entire first floor would probably be around $1,000," he told me.

"Not bad," I thought to myself. I took his card and told him I would reach out if I decided not to do it myself. That night, I sat in a metal folding chair in the middle of our living room turning over his business card in my hand. I took a look around at the walls. "I'm not gonna pay him; I can just do this myself," I thought to myself. I threw his card in our kitchen drawer and headed to Home Depot to pick up supplies. I told a Home Depot employee about my painting project and asked what supplies I would need.

I spent the next hour following the Home Depot representative around the store, throwing item after item into my cart. Rolling brushes, three different-sized paint brushes, paint trays, painter's tape, tarps, buckets, edging tools, and the list goes on. Finally, it was time to pick out my paint color. I had looked up what color paint I wanted online. My wife and I wanted a similar gray color to the gray that was already on the walls. I provided the name of the color to the representative in the paint section, and they mixed a few cans for me. As I hurriedly did some quick research online before going to Home Depot, I read that you should also get a primer to put on the walls before painting. I purchased a few cans of primer. I walked out of Home Depot with six bags of supplies and a receipt totaling around $500.

The next day I started work painting the room. It took two hours of taping around the trim and windows to understand the full scope of the project I had embarked on. The first day was filled with frustrations of tape not laying straight and more primer ending up on my clothes than the walls. After the first full day, I was about halfway done priming the walls. By the end of the second day, I had finished priming all of the walls. I now had a fresh white canvas to start painting. Day three was a blur of edging trim and rolling walls.

Nonstop up and down from a step stool painting one section of the room after another.

Positioning the tarp, painting a section, repositioning, painting. Over and over again until it was dark out. By the end of the day, I had finished half of the first floor. I woke up the next day and looked at my progress so far. A pit grew in my stomach as I saw the white from the primer was showing through the first coat of paint. I then discovered a costly error in my plan of attack. Because I was using a similar gray to the original gray paint, I did not need to use a primer. I definitely should have not used a white primer. This meant I was going to have to do three layers total, including the layer of primer—one layer of primer and two layers of paint to cover up the white.

I walked to the kitchen, opened the first drawer on the left of our cabinets, reached inside, and grabbed the handyman's business card. I looked at the smile of the handyman on the card and vowed to never make this mistake again. After three more days of painting, I had finished the first level of our house. It took me seven full days and $750 in total cost to paint the first level of our house. I saved $250 doing it myself at the cost of seven days neglecting my business, seven days of frustration, and seven days of tough work.

I learned a valuable lesson that day: Don't waste time to save money. While I saved $250, I wasted seven days I could have spent earning eight times that by focusing on my business. I could have saved myself from this entire debacle had I focused on the "Who Not How" principle.

How We Can Help

Who Not How is a best-selling book by Dan Sullivan and Benjamin Hardy that focuses on the importance of figuring out "who" can help you achieve your goals instead of "how" you are going to do it alone.[19] Time is our most precious resource. We can never get more time. Videography University can be the "who" to help you save time, money, and frustration on your journey to building your videography business to a six-figure Income. I learned thousands of lessons the hard way over seven years of building my videography business to six figures. My mission is to help other videographers skip the trial and error and go farther, quicker with their business. I don't want it to take you seven years to hit the $100,000-mark, I want to help you get there in 10 to 12 months.

Videography University is an online coaching program where my team and I work alongside you to help you grow your videography business. Videography University consists of one-on-one coaching, online training videos, group coaching, a private Facebook Group with other videographers where you can ask questions and learn from those on the same journey as you, and much more. If you are serious about taking the next step in growing your videography business, whether that be as a part-time job or your full-time career, schedule a free call with my team at www.videography-university.com/apply.

On this call we'll talk with you about your business to see if Videography University is a good fit for you. If it's a good fit, we'll walk you through the next steps to getting you on your way to growing your videography business to a six-figure Income. Our mission is to help 1,000 videographers accomplish the goal of earning a $100,000 income with their business and ultimately live a richer, more fulfilling life. Have you ever heard the saying, "The best time to plant a tree was 20 years ago. The second-best time is now"?

Don't waste any more time. The best next step to build your videography business is to book a call with us right now. Go to www.videography-university.com/apply, and lock in a call with us today.

Endnotes

1. Coelho, P. (2014). *The Alchemist*. HarperOne.

2. Alouani, N. (2021, September 5). *Accountability — Or how to give yourself a 95% chance of achieving your goal*. Medium. https://2madness.com/accountability-or-how-to-give-yourself-a-95-chance-of-achieving-your-goal-f972b4ae27ce

3. Bondarenko, P., & Petruzzello, M. (2023, May 4). *Starbucks*. Encyclopedia Britannica. https://www.britannica.com/topic/Starbucks

4. Hall, M. (2023, May 9). *Amazon.com*. Encyclopedia Britannica. https://www.britannica.com/topic/Amazoncom; Morano, H. F. (2023, May 2). *From A to Z: The complete history of Amazon*. EcomCrew. https://www.ecomcrew.com/from-a-to-z-the-complete-history-of-amazon-com/

5. Haslam, K. (2020, March 5). *Why is Apple called Apple?* Macworld. https://www.macworld.com/article/673923/why-is-apple-called-apple.html

6. Morano, *From A to Z: The complete history of Amazon*.

7. Zabalkanska, H. (2019, July 16). *7 most effective ways to increase the response rate of your emails five times.* Newoldstamp. https://newoldstamp. com/blog/ most-effective-ways-to-increase-the-response-rate-of-your-emails-five-times/

8. Wyzowl. (n.d.). *Testimonial statistics 2020.* https://www. wyzowl.com/testimonials-statistics/

9. Gallo, A. (2014, October 29). *The value of keeping the right customers.* Harvard Business Review. https://hbr.org/2014/10/ the-value-of-keeping-the-right-customers

10. Newswire. (2012, April). *Consumer trust in online, social and mobile advertising grows.* Nielsen. https://www. nielsen.com/insights/2012/consumer-trust-in-online-social-and-mobile-advertising-grows/

11. Movsisyan, A. (2021, December 8). *Video marketing statistics.* Yans Media. https://www.yansmedia.com/ blog/video-marketing-statistics

12. Georgiev, D. (2023, February 28). *How much time do people spend on social media in 2023?* Techjury. https://techjury.net/blog/ time-spent-on-social-media/#gref

13. Iyengar, S. S., & Lepper, M. R. (2000). When choice is demotivating: Can one desire too much of a good thing? *Journal of Personality and Social Psychology, 79*(6), 995–1006. https://doi.org/10.1037//0022-3514.79.6.995

14. Duarte, N. (2022, December 20). *10 ways to prepare for a TED style talk.* Duarte. https://www.duarte.com/10-ways-to-prepare-for-a-ted-format-talk/

15. Saleh, K. (2019, November 11). *Customer acquisition vs. retention costs.* Invesp. https://www.invespcro.com/blog/customer-acquisition-retention/

16. Hill, N. (2011). *The law of success in sixteen lessons.* Wilder Publications.

17. Delzio, S. (2015, June 9). 12 social media marketing trends for small business. Social Media Examiner. https://www.socialmediaexaminer.com/social-media-marketing-trends-for-small-business/

18. Yaqub, M. (2023, April 4). *How many businesses use social media: State of social media for business (2023 Update).* BusinessDIT. https://www.businessdit.com/social-media-for-business-statistics/

19. Sullivan, D., & Hardy, B. (2020). *Who Not How: The Formula to Achieve Bigger Goals Through Accelerating Teamwork*. Hay House, Inc.

20. Hopkins, Tom. (2015). *How to Master the Art of Selling*. Made For Success Publishing.

Acknowledgments

I would be remiss to not send a special thank you to all who helped me write this book. First, I want to thank my family. To my wife, Kristin, thank you for putting up with all of the late nights, long weekends, and early mornings that I spent writing this book. Your sacrifice helped to make this book possible. Thank you for also believing in me. Your support of my dreams is what allowed me to build a career out of my passion. I love you. To my parents, thank you for your constant support in life. You are both the model of hard work and perseverance, and I don't know where I would be today if it weren't for you. To my brother and sister, thank you for paving the way for me in life. I was the lucky one who got to sit back and learn from both of you as I journeyed through life. Thank you for being the best big brother and big sister a little brother could ask for.

Now, for my friends who played a special role in helping me on my journey of building a career out of this passion of mine. Kyler Holland, without you, none of this would be possible. You were the catalyst to the start of my videography career. You equipped me with the tools, gave me access to the knowledge, and provided me with the confidence to pursue this passion of mine. My only hope is that this book can pay it forward to provide others with half the help you gave me. To Ryan Willis, thank you for being my accountability partner on this journey. Your support, advice, and encouragement has helped me overcome many obstacles. I am indebted to you for this. To all of my other friends not mentioned specifically, you know who you are, and I thank you for all of the support you have provided me in life. Your support in times of need, your ear when I needed someone to listen, and your shoulder when I needed someone to lean on played an important role in helping me get to where I am today. Thank you. I also want to thank my editor, Nancy Pile, for crossing my T's and dotting my I's. Your expertise and skills brought this book to life. Lastly, I want to thank my launch team for providing your feedback, support, and experience. Your feedback was instrumental in putting the finishing touches on this book and, in turn, helping change the lives of many aspiring videographers.

Author Bio

Grant Burks is the owner and operator of Optiko Productions, a videography business. Now he runs Videography University, an online school where he teaches aspiring videographers how to realize their dreams of building a full-time career in videography. Grant posts free videography-related content and tutorials on all of his social media channels. You can follow Grant on Instagram @grantburk_vu, on YouTube @grantburks, and on Twitter @grantburks_vu.

URGENT PLEA!

Thank You for Reading My Book!

I really appreciate all of your feedback and
I love hearing what you have to say.
I need your input to make the next version of this
book and my future books better.

Please take two minutes now to leave a helpful review on
Amazon, letting me know what you thought of the book:
filmtofreedom.com/review
Thanks so much!
—Grant Burks